Confessions of a Feng Shui Ghost-Buster

Release Spirits, Souls and Supernatural Forces Using Feng Shui

By

Anna Maria Prezio

ISBN 978-1-4357-0640-8

To Order a Copy of this Book, visit:

www.fengshuiharmony.net

www.annamariaprezio.com

or

www.prezio.com

DISCLAIMER

The information contained in this book, *Confessions of a Feng Shui Ghost-Buster,* and the author(s), Anna Maria Prezio, is for the sole purpose of education and reference material. It is in no way intended as medical advice. Before employing any method, consult with your physician and/or the advice of an expert. The methods and techniques described are intended as an extension and supplement to knowledge and education in the Art of Feng Shui and other Asian Studies and Philosophies. The authors are not responsible in any way for any damage or injuries sustained to property(s) or person(s) that may occur by employing technique, methods or instructions contained in this book.

Praise for *Confessions of a Feng Shui Ghost-Buster*

"Anna Maria's easy-to-read book on how to release ghosts is upbeat and full of insights. This book is well worth the read. She mixes the old with the new in an intelligent way."

– Pam Case
Chinese Astrologer and Intuitive

"The author skillfully balances the serious business of ghost removal with lighthearted tales of her European heritage. Its simply written and fascinating with personal experiences and clear instructions that will surely guide you to understand the process."

– C.P. Henry
Design Director

"This book, *Confessions of a Feng Shui Ghost-Buster,* is for the person who likes to take matters into their own hands.........to be in control of their world!!! Anna Maria's insights to 'taking charge' are so very helpful. Her writing is easy to understand. With the feng shui approach you get clarity and purity."

– Victoria Burrows
Casting Director for Film and Television

"Anna Maria and I share great passion for feng shui and the removal of ghosts, Anna Maria's new book is a must have for anyone who realizes the power of 'Positive' energy."

– Dan McBee
C.E.O Whisper International

"Finally someone has written a book about ghosts that is helpful and charming without being hokey. The combination of real world experience with academic study makes for a great read. Curl up with some of that tea I hear so much about and enjoy."

– Ramsey Moore
Actor

Dedication

Mamma

Acknowledgements

Special thanks to my son, Anthony, for his appreciation, brilliance, encouragement and love.

Thanks to my sister, Clara, for her insight and support.

Gratitude to all my teachers, friends, colleagues, mentors, guides and God.

Thanks to my wonderful trusting clients.

Special thanks to Carma Spence-Pothitt, my talented editor, whose creativity is endless.

Table of Contents

About the Author

Anna Maria Prezio is a Certified Feng Shui Consultant and Intuitive. She has studied with a multitude of feng shui masters and metaphysical gurus. She has devoted herself to helping others achieve optimum positive environmental energies. She has done this through hundreds of feng shui audits, readings and consultations on a local, national and international level. She teaches, lectures and writes on feng shui and metaphysical subjects.

She received her BA in communications from Villanova University as well as a Business Graduate degree. Her expertise is in the communication arts, visual arts, and entrepreneurship. She is a certified entrepreneurship instructor for the Executive Entrepreneur Institute and has held executive positions in marketing for multi-national corporations. She has incorporated her knowledge of feng shui and its effects on personal environments to enhance people's lives.

Anna Maria's mission is to help people gain the knowledge and tools of feng shui to improve and enhance their wealth, health, creativity and relationships.

Ms. Prezio' experience, feng shui knowledge and intuitive talent give her the ability to sense people, places and things which help to nurture and facilitate her client's lifestyles.

Her clients include people from all walks of life.

About the Book

This non-traditional book is intended to explain in a no nonsense and fearless manner ways in which the reader can be involved in seeing feng shui as a tool for clearing their environment to release supernatural forces, souls and spirits using feng shui principles.

It is my story on how I became a metaphysician, feng shui principals that are easy to master and cases involving actual ghost-busting. Balancing and harmonizing your environment is critical to a happy, joyful and productive individual. Physical and emotional wellbeing are the key to living and maintaining an abundant and prosperous life.

Forward

As a registered nurse, an Interfaith Minister and a metaphysician, I have had the unique opportunity to interact with many different people from all different walks of life and in a variety of situations including friendships, patients in my practice, hospitals, hospice, ministry and corporate America. Grounded in science, yet having evolved to being a more conscious and aware individual through my studies in Metaphysics, my diverse and sometimes paradoxical background has afforded me the ability to see the bigger picture – the plethora of experiences that constitute life on this planet in human form.

What has intrigued me even more, however, have been the experiences that have been communicated to me when an opening of safety was created where the client/friend/colleague felt comfortable communicating an unconventional or unusual occurrence that was outside the realm of the expected and typical experiences of what we call "reality." The desire to share the experience is unfortunately usually overshadowed by the worry of what people will think and how it will be interpreted when such an experience is communicated or shared.

Metaphysically, however, we are constantly "reading" each other's energy and if we believe, as I do, that there are no coincidences and that people and situations come into our life for a reason, it is a great blessing to run into someone of like open-mindedness, who energetically invites us to share a mystical experience with acceptance and interest.

What I have been learning is that these are the experiences that connect us more fully with the unity and oneness that we are – not just what we do here on the planet, but who we truly are. They are the experiences of the spirit – the soul, both individual and collective, and ultimately of the Divine. They also allow us to know that we are not alone in our experiences both common and mystical and enable us to become more compassionate and understanding toward ourselves and toward each other.

Part I of *Confessions of a Feng Shui Ghost-Buster* captures your attention with a ghostly first experience of an intuitive and vulnerable 6 year-old child. The culture and experiences of the author growing up in a rural and mystical village in Italy where ghostly occurrences and stories were part of every day life serve to set the stage for what would be a life long study of the mystical and the Divine.

Part II describes feng shui, like medicine, as both an art and a science. Here, the definitions and different sects of feng shui are discussed so as to provide a backdrop for the connection between environmental balance and the appearance of ghosts. And like the esoteric aspects of religion that are hidden in the stones and structures of cathedrals and temples, and the deeper meanings of nature and life that are veiled in the Vedas as poetry, mastery of feng shui helps us to understand the occult or hidden knowledge as it applies to all aspects of our life here on earth.

With the formation of a solid foundation and understanding of this art and science, Part III delves deeper into the correlation between environment and entities with ideas, cures and stories about ghost busting as a result the author's direct and extraordinary experience.

This remarkable practice is not just about moving things around in the house, but as I have observed personally and professionally, it is really consciousness that is moving as in, as above, so below, and as within so without. Just like a clear mind will invite you to desire a clean desk, cleaning up your desk will inevitably invite a clear mind. It matters not with what or where you start. Energy will move regardless, and it is with this intent that ghost busting is undertaken to improve health, well-being, finances, and relationships. By adjusting the environment so as to create and invite harmony, balance and peace here on earth, we can assist the departed with going on to their rightful and restful place in the universe where we will all one day meet again as One.

Everything in the universe is energy and although we are seemingly living in a material world, Quantum Physics has proven time and time again that even the material is not really material or solid. Even our thoughts, words, deeds and intent are energy or Chi (Chinese) or Prana (Indian). Isn't the well-known scientific fact that energy is neither created nor destroyed enough proof for the existence of consciousness after we die? That ever-present witnessing awareness with thoughts, feelings, emotions and personality continues even after the physical body has stopped functioning. And if you have doubts about this undying awareness, as you are reading this, turn your attention to the one who is doing the reading.

Our tendency to want to explain away these experiences with flimsy and exclusively scientific justification denies the mystery of life that also needs to be honored as much as that which we seemingly think we know for sure. When we share these encounters, we also learn that these experiences are consistent across cultures and are much like the common threads of love and compassion that run throughout all religions and traditions. When we open our minds and hearts to understand at this level, we open ourselves to the feeling of unity that resides within each of us.

Written with thoughtfulness, clarity and immense compassion for both the ghost or entity and those being haunted, *Confessions of a Feng Shui Ghost-Buster* will intrigue, delight and capture you as you journey with the author through her knowledge and experiences where the price of admission is an open mind to not only better understand ourselves, but the metaphysical world in which we live forever.

— Rev. Dr. Joanna M. Carmichael
Heart 2 Heart Creative Healing and Consulting, Inc.
Newtown Square, PA
December 2007

Introduction

Some of us have seen ghosts ... but won't tell.

Some of us who have seen ghosts, what them to go away ... others want them to stay.

Some of us who have seen ghosts won't leave their homes ... others are afraid, but still keep them.

Some of us want to see ghosts again and again, to connect with their world ... others don't know how to get rid of them, even if they want to.

Some of those who have not seen ghosts want to ... others are merely intrigued by the idea that they exist.

And then, some people do not believe in ghosts at all.

Whether or not you believe in ghosts, have seen ghosts, or have wanted to get rid of them or not, you will appreciate ghost stories and how to get rid of ghosts.

Releasing, removing or "busting" ghosts is sometimes a very difficult task that should only be undertaken by an expert. There are such experts.

I wrote this book to guide you step by step and effortlessly on how to get rid of unwanted entities. I know first hand that many of us have had similar experiences and feared speaking about it. Telling someone that you've seen a ghost could have unwanted consequences. I wanted to reassure you that this is not an unnatural experience but quite common. Some have asked me, 'aren't you afraid to do what you do?' I can assure you that I am not, for fear is false evidence appearing real. The more we know and understand about what we fear the easier it is to accept a solution.

I have many solutions for my varied clients. Their experiences, though unique, are very real. My job is to alleviate the client's concerns and to remove the nuisance that lingers and is annoying the individuals or community. We all have the right to peace and serenity. Our home is our castle. If we feel safe, secure and serene then we can move forward to good health, wealth and prosperity. This is my mission and my passion.

You might ask yourself, "In today's society, do ghosts really exist?" They do, because people report them. They do exist, because there are sightings and cases of ghosts that were disruptive to the homeowners. Some tolerated them for far too long, without saying a word to anyone.

This book will show you that it is possible to release and clear ghosts, entities and spirits and how to create a peaceful environment for yourself so that your home can be a sanctuary -- something we all deserve to have. Our home is our refuge, our harbor and our retreat.

This book will show you that it is possible to clear unwanted spirits, even if they are particularly challenging. Sometimes certain ghosts are difficult to rid of, but once they know that you do not want them around and that they belong in another place, they will go.

It sometimes takes several tries to get them out, and sometimes it takes more expertise. If these entities are troublesome -- and even if they are not -- they do not belong on the earthly plane. They have a place where they belong and they need to be there, not on earth and in your house. Sometimes they are in buildings other than your house, such as offices, factories and guesthouses or trailers. They are where they were left and they inhabit the strangest of places.

When we ask them to leave we are doing them a big favor. They don't know it at the time but they deserve to be where they belong and that is that place that is waiting for them on the other side or in another dimension. Where they are going is the right

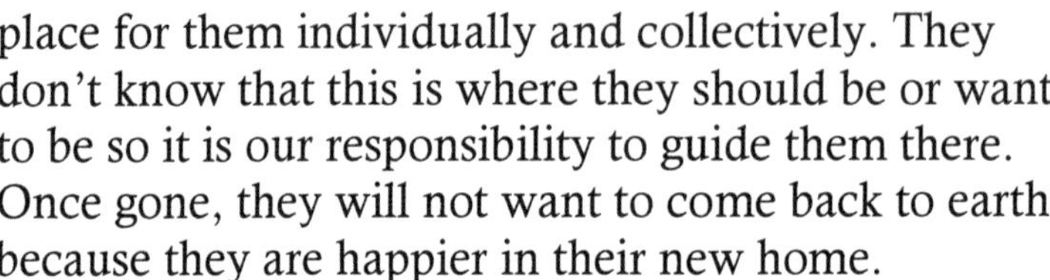

place for them individually and collectively. They don't know that this is where they should be or want to be so it is our responsibility to guide them there. Once gone, they will not want to come back to earth because they are happier in their new home.

They could inhabit a new home. It could be a shed, a garage or a guesthouse where they spent some of their time. I knew of one entity that moved to the garage where he spent lots of time working with his tools on his hobby. He moved there even after the main house was cleared. No one knew for quite some time. Some ghosts are just that stubborn. In this case another clearing had to be done. He was guided out. Once they are gone for good and are not inhabiting another structure, they will be much happier with their environment. They will not want to come back.

It's up to you. Do you want them to stay or do you want them to leave and leave for good? Only you can answer this question.

If you want them to leave there are techniques that will give them that needed nudge to leave this earthly plane. Once they leave and find their appropriate afterlife residence they will not want to return. If, on the other hand, you don't want them to leave you are doing them a disservice. They are not happy in a limbo state. As time moves on, they can become an even more disruptive and destructive force.

If you have decided to help them leave you need to know how to do it. Either hire someone who has the expertise in clearing and releasing ghosts and entities or you can attempt to do it yourself. Some are squeamish at the thought of communicating with a ghost in any way and others don't mind the job. If you are one of those people who don't mind, there are a few simple things you can do to help them leave your premises. The instructions in the subsequent chapters are taken directly from actual ghost releasing that I performed in client's houses to rid them of unwanted spirits and ghosts. These entities are no longer on this plane. They have been released and cleared. They are now in a better, happier and rightful place.

This book is intended as a guide through the process of leading spirits, ghosts and entities to that rightful place.

PART ONE:

My Journey

Chapter 1: Spirits

I felt my warm blanket being pulled off me and, suddenly, a hurtful slap on my behind. It startled me awake. I was a terrified 6-year-old. It was All Saint's Eve in a small village town in Italy. Everyone invited the spirits of their dead relatives to visit them. Glasses of wine and plates of food were left for visiting spirits. My small bed was placed in the dining room where my family members thought the spirits would enter. They even left the front door open for them, as this was the custom. I was afraid, but told no one. I remained very still, but my heart was racing and the seemingly large, cold hand that struck me with only one blow never returned.

It was not a dream and it was not imagined. To this day, I have told only a few people. They wanted to comfort me, so they made excuses. They would say, "It was a prank" or "Maybe it was a joke by your siblings." One person even said, "You may have had a very active imagination then." After all, it was Halloween night. As a young child remembers things in their past, some things are unforgettable. This was one of those incidents. Why would I repeat anything that may have been mocked or

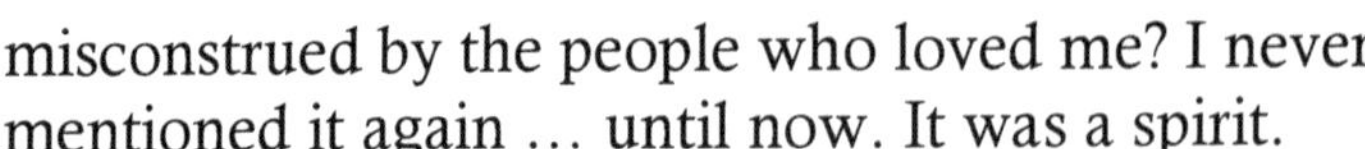

misconstrued by the people who loved me? I never mentioned it again … until now. It was a spirit.

My grandfather used to tell me ghost stories when I was a little girl. Story telling was the only entertainment there was in that small village in southern Italy. No television. No radio. And hardly any books to read to keep our active minds occupied. At the end of the day, we would gather around the brasciere, a large container made from brass or copper, filled with coal for warmth and heat during cold winter months. It was the only heater, except for our rustic fireplace. We would gather around the brasciere and listen to the stories being told. Some were folklore and others were thought to be real. Very scary for a young imagination to absorb. My grandfather, Vincenzo, was the best at telling spooky stories. Every sound was amplified. He became animated. At the end of the story it was hard to fall asleep.

Our house was a large two-story. It was built by my grandparents, Mamma's mother and father. They lived downstairs. This is where I slept, because it was too crowded on the second floor. We were a large family of seven. I actually enjoyed having the entire dining room to myself and I didn't have to share a bed with any of my sisters. I felt like a princess. My grandparents gave me lots of attention. Can't say I didn't like it.

This was the house where I was born, and grew up in until almost age 8 when my family left Italy to travel to the US. It belonged to my mother and father. They bought the house from Momma's parents. In the Italian tradition, parents left their houses to their daughters. The two daughters, my mother Maria and her sister Filippina, would have possession of the house and keep it in the family unless one sister would sell to the other.

My mother bought her sister's share at a time when her sister was having financial difficulty. My aunt was grateful that my mother offered to buy her share. The money my father earned was always placed directly in my mother's hands. Mamma was frugal. She knew how to stretch a lira. She set aside a small amount from their earnings. She had saved enough to make the purchase. She paid 250,000 lire for the house. In 1939, that amount was equal to approximately $2,500 US.

Onc day my father came home from a long day working at the annual carnival miles away from home. He was the only photographer in the region. He photographed couples, children, even priests and nuns. He would travel on his bicycle, sometimes 80 miles, to bordering towns to set up his camera equipment at the fiera annuale. Each day, when he came home, he gave my mother the day's earnings, as usual.

She sat him down as if something very important was going to be said and told him that the house now belonged to them. She showed him the deed. He got very excited! He jumped up and said, "Maria, you made me the happiest man alive. How did you do it?"

Every time Mamma told the story, she would get very animated and you could see from her face how much love she had for my papa. She spoke about how he picked her up and swung her in the air and twirled her around. My mom was almost five feet tall, if that, and my father was almost six feet tall. She felt like she was on top of the world. The way he lifted her, as she told it, was as if she was crowned queen. He placed her on that pedestal that women crave. She felt his love, his respect, his devotion and affection in one fell swoop. She told me that she felt so much love from her husband that day that nothing could compare to it. I can still hear her tell that story. Any of my sisters or brother will tell you this story in the exact same way.

My grandfather, Vincenzo, was a gentle soul. He spoke softly. He seemed very tall to me. He had white hair, blue eyes and was light skinned like my Mamma. He taught me how to count in English. He had been to America, but frowned upon any one of his immediate family members moving there, because of the hardship he endured. He knew that no matter what he said, someday, we would follow in his footsteps.

In Roggiano Gravina everyone knew each other. Everyone told ghost stories, even my father. They called him Maestro Angiolino. He served in the Italian army during World War II as bandleader for his battalion in Tripoli. Even though my father had made a name for himself as the only photographer, and the only music teacher of his time, in this small village, he wanted to journey to America to make a better life for his family.

My uncle Salvatore, my father's brother, was a successful man in America, or so we thought. Uncle Sal was one of the reasons why my father left Italy for Philadelphia. As it turned out, Uncle Sal was a cabinetmaker foreman, and had a house with a white picket fence in an Irish neighborhood, much like everyone else on the block. When papa left for the US, we missed his ghost stories. That's when my grandfather took over and embellished on the scariest of stories, especially when told in the dimness of night.

I wanted to stay up and listen to all of them and hear every small detail. I did not want him to skip a beat. Nonno did not like interruptions, and so he commanded a silent audience.

One night in front of the fire when I would not listen to my mother's request to go to bed, my slumber took over. Slowly but surely as I was sitting straight up in my chair, I fell right into the fire, palms up, into the burning hot coal. The palms of my small hands were severely burned. The pain was excruciating. It felt like a million stab wounds. The skin was charred and ready to fall off. My screams woke everyone out of their sleep.

My mother, our neighbors, and even my Zia Mara, heard my screams and rushed right over. Auntie lived two houses away. No sooner did she show up, than she ran right back out to pluck several large leaves from a nearby large plant called cento nervi, which means one hundred nerves. She dampened and placed these large green leaves over my palms.

She knew immediately what to do. She wrapped my hands with gauze to keep the leaves in place and told me to be still. Mamma brewed a cup of chamomile tea to calm me down. Shosha Annita, our next door neighbor sat with me to make sure I was OK. She was like a mother to all of us. The very next day the burning was gone, and so was the pain. No scars were left on either palm.

From that point on, Nonno was not going to allow me to stay up late. He liked having an audience, but had to modify his schedule … and mine. Needless to say I was sadly disappointed.

Chapter 2: Ancestors

One of the reasons why there were so many ghost stories to tell is simply because, in a small village town, for the most part people died in their homes, generation after generation. Hospitals and clinics were not easily accessible and people were cared for in their own homes by their families.

When a family member died it was usually at home, with their loved ones around them. There was often a priest, usually there to give last rites, Extreme Unction. Their spirits either crossed over peacefully or they were detained from leaving this earthly plain for one reason or another.

There were so many stories to tell because it was commonplace to see ghosts, even if they were given a proper burial. Ghost stories were a part of many conversations.

My interest in ghost stories started even before the story telling. I remember seeing my father's father, sitting in a chair in my Nonno's dark bedroom. Also named Vincenzo, he had died in his early 50s before I was born. He also had nothing good to say about his adventures to America. After all, he came to the US during the depression, a time when people were standing in soup lines and many people lost their jobs, money and homes.

The United States was devastated by the Great Depression of 1929. This event also occurred throughout the world during World War II, mostly due to the effects of international trade. Everyone was in debt. After the depression came a recession and recovery was long and hard in coming.

My father did everything he could to feed his family. He traveled on his bicycle to surrounding towns taking photographs at fairs and weddings. He even made wooden shoes to support his growing family after the war. He took on woodworking projects and created a niche as a carpenter, photographer and music teacher.

In those days after World War II, people throughout Italy did whatever they could to survive. The psychological affects of post war took its toll. Most people feared for their future and were reluctant to add new debt. From 1950 onward, European economic growth was rapid and therefore world trade helped recovery with foreign aid. In 1954 my father decided that the best future was to move to the US. Mamma saved for that, too. Two years later, after he had established himself, the rest of his family followed. We were reunited. We now had a house with a white picket fence.

Chapter 3: See-ers

My father continued to tell us stories of people he had known who channeled other spirits. He didn't call it that, but I've come to know it as channeling. These were not just ghost stories. They were stories of the supernatural, and of spirits inhabiting other's bodies, such as playing an instrument as if the player was in a trance and it was known that he had never had any musical training of any type.

I just wished that I had written down all these stories. They were uncensored, and did not seem to be made up at all. Some of these people were town people who knew my father. They all knew him. He was a playful kind of guy.

One story told to me was of an old woman who sent for my father. She had been very ill and was immobile. She wanted him to go to her house and get a violin that was hanging near the doorway. He followed her instructions. When he first saw her in her bedroom she sat up and was speaking in her husband's voice. He saw that she had been possessed by her dead husband's spirit. He brought the musical instrument to her. She took it in her hands and adjusted it under her chin as if she had done this a million times. She started to play it like a professional and played it beautifully.

As my father told this particular story, he said he had never heard an instrument played that well in his life. He said that when she stopped playing it, she handed the instrument to my father and smiled. She then lay on her bed, closed her eyes and moments later she died peacefully.

He was not certain what all that entailed, but he knew for certain that it was not the old woman playing that instrument. It was the spirit of her dead husband wanting to help her cross over. That was my father's explanation of that event. This ghost story stayed with me.

Years later, I told my father what I had seen. He was not surprised. He's the one who told me that it was his father whom I saw. I had described him as having a handlebar mustache and a full head of hair. Papa knew that I could see his dead father. At that time I had no idea how much of an impact this would have on my life. Certain incidences and events that took place, particularly as a child, would stay with me, unexplained, mostly because I feared telling anyone. What child wants to be laughed at? As I got older I understood the power that comes with being intuitive, sensing and understanding people's head chatter and emotions. I actually thought that everyone could do this and be what and how I am.

My parents told me many times that, as a young child, I was never afraid of the dark. I don't know if my mother was exaggerating when she said I was two years old and getting up in the middle of the night to go to the bathroom by myself. Unlike her other children, I was the only one who was not afraid of the dark. Growing up, I was fearless. I was not afraid of people, places and things. My imagination was fertile. If I put my mind to it, anything at all that I wanted to do was a done deal.

Children can see entities more easily and more often than adults can. If you watch a child interact, you will notice that they choose to go to places where they feel a strong energy.

It was not until later in my life that all of this became clear and, somewhat, unscrambled. As metaphysical professions began to become more mainstream, and as popularity allowed it all to surface, I did not give my talents the stigma that once kept it a secret. As time went on I accepted my metaphysical acumen and expected it to rise to the surface. I allowed myself to share it with others. Some people saw my ability without speaking a word.

Chapter 4: Body Language

I was at an impressionable age when I came to the US, not knowing how to speak English – except for "one," "two" and "three." The one thing that I relied on was body language, and my own made up sign language – or, you could call it signaling. Motions like "stop" or "listen" or "sit" or "stand" were easily interpreted visually.

It was not easy for a child to be thrown into a culture that is not understandable. I had to learn how to communicate non-verbally very quickly. I knew what people were trying to say to me just by watching them. Soon, I became an expert in body language. I knew a range of emotions and inflections that did not need a word attached to it. I could understand tonality, and even felt a vibrational energy from people.

It got easier and better to just nod "yes" or "no." Within a couple of months I was able to learn words, phrases and even short sentences. My first book was *Dick and Jane.* I had difficulty removing the Italian vowel sounds. It sort of sounded like 'Deek end Jen' but eventually, I was not laughed at in school and other children grew fond of my quirky way of speaking. In fact, they loved me as a novelty.

They wanted me to be in line with them and gave me candy, which I never turned down, and they even wanted to carry my bag. That only lasted until I knew my way around and I became "one of them."

I was struggling with niceties. I was on good behavior. I imagined terrible things would happen to me if I did not behave. Why?

As a young 6-year-old student, I used to carry a school bag that I loved because it looked like a doctor's bag, the old type that doctors used when they made home visits. Yes, doctors in those days used to make house calls. I carried the bag everywhere and thought that someday that was what I would end up doing.

My first day back in school I returned with a workbook full of crayon scribble that my little sister entertained herself with the night before. My teacher called me up to the front of the classroom and started saying things to me in a higher pitched tone. She kept pointing to the Crayola crayoned book in an angry tone. Her face contorted a bit and then pointed her index finger at me. I knew that the workbook was meant for me to study and to work out my math problems. The other students in the class were so quiet you could hear a pin drop. I could feel all those little eyes on me. My face felt as if it was burning, and I must have turned beet red. I felt very embarrassed. I could not defend myself nor explain that I did not intentionally destroy my workbook. She was not interested in any of that, and sent me back to sit at my desk. That I understood loud and clear. I could not even look at another classmate. I felt such humiliation and stupidity.

The other children did not laugh at all. They also felt it. I never told on my sister. I thought one humiliation that day was enough. This is the kind of disaster I would want to avoid at all costs, so I tried from that day forward to lay very low, not make noise and be a "good student."

As time went by it got easier. I was determined not just to learn the English language, but to master it.

Chapter 5: Honor Thy Intuition

After moving to California in the early '90s, I found myself struggling with career choices. I saw an ad for an entrepreneurship course being offered to anyone who had been let go of his or her high-powered job. I interviewed for the government-funded course and took the required placement test that was basically set up to see whether or not I would match the established criteria for "entrepreneur."

The test is best known as the Myers Briggs Inventory Test, which provides a personality assessment formula describing your type description specifically designed for career choices. The results of my tests were high in regards to intuition, feeling, sensing and judging. This test can measure whether you are an extravert or an introvert. It's an indicator that helps with career decision and is often used by career human resources professionals for job placement and by college counselors to help students with their career decision process. I found out that I am a futuristic thinker who perceives through intuition.

After seeing the results of my test, the founder of this prestigious entrepreneur program knew that my personality type was uncommon. After taking the course, he invited me to become one of three directors of the program. The mission of the program was to expand it and to educate and teach entrepreneurial skills so that students could start and grow a business.

Students enrolled in the program were professionals who had been downsized or displaced, mostly aerospace engineers. Structuring the curriculum and teaching were among my duties. I was to determine who could enter the program based on their history, test results information and my ability to analyze potential recruits. Those eligible would have the potential of forming a successful company. I had the final say in who could enter this six-month, accelerated learning program, using test results and interviews as measures.

My boss, knowing that I had the skills to make this judgment, was also looking for funding to support these newly created businesses. He would ask me to sit in on the meetings with venture capitalists and assess whether or not they would be viable in procuring the necessary funds. Would these people who said they had money actually have the funding or were they exploiting our students to get ideas?

I was accurate every time. I was the genuine 'Counselor Deanna Troi', the *Star Trek* empath able to read emotions and sense what was happening around her. As the TV series character, she would advise the captain in a variety of situations because she was innately wise, and intuitively had extensive knowledge in philosophy, psychology and religions.

I was taking on this empathic role among an all male staff, running a program that consisted of mostly male students. In the early '90s, it was still a male-dominated work force. Studies show that more men than women lack in the intuition department, so I gained a lot of respect from my peers through the validation of my outstanding talent of intuitive acumen, and knowing how to use it. This yielded power and comfort at the same time.

Having unique abilities is an aphrodisiac. The power of intuition is greater than any other power I have known. By that I mean the competitive edge that we need to assist us in our endeavors. It doesn't mean that I diminish the power of love, sex or even power itself, but that it enhances all other powers that I have or know about. I knew that, at this point in my life, grasping this talent that is not so common after all would be an enhancement in every facet of my life. The question continued to be "Now what?"

Chapter 6: Metaphysician

It took several more years of reading books to realize that I was headed toward the metaphysical realm of study and practice. When I was in college, if someone was to tell me that I would be working in metaphysics, I would have laughed at them. If someone would have told me this while I was heading corporations, restructuring marketing divisions and creating new marketing campaigns for multi-national corporations, I would have told them that they were crazy. I'm not doing that! I'm not that!

Well, I came to my awakening and understanding of my talents. It was a long journey of detours to find it and myself.

The idea of metaphysical study slowly trickled in as a hobby. My intelligent, creative and beautiful sister, Clara, started it all. She gave me a book on feng shui about 20 years ago. I had never heard these two words before. The more I read, the more I wanted to know more and more.

To regress somewhat, a friend of mine told me about an astrologer who was teaching astrology at

Temple University. She had a session with him and found him to be very accurate.

Twenty years ago, few people sought the counsel of an astrologer, and if you did it was kept very hush-hush.

I made my appointment.

At that time, paying anyone to read your future was something you thought twice about. He was not what and who I thought he would be. He did not have a turban on his head, nor did he have a crystal ball to gaze into. I found him to be very intelligent and focused. He spoke in a direct and staccato tone. He talked about the past, the present and the future. When he got to the future he told me that I would have a home based business in a metaphysical career, because I was highly psychic and intuitive.

I laughed.

He stopped what he was doing and looked at me. I, too, realized that I was laughing at him. Oops!

He actually said, "I'm one of them. I teach at a prestigious University. I have a PhD and I'm the best there is at what I do. Do you have any questions?"

Well, I was sorry for offending him. He was giving me some amazing news about myself and I was not willing to accept his gift. Though he understood, he knew that I would some day come to the realization of what this revelation would mean to me. I've thought about him many times after that first meeting. He went to Russia shortly after our meeting where he is highly esteemed. Dr. Jacob Schwartz is known around the world for his contributions in astrology and asteroids. His interpretations and predictions turned out to be very accurate.

Photo Album

Franco, Clara, Anna Maria (age 6) and Carmela

Prezio family portrait
Anna Maria (age 5), lower right

Carolina and Vincenzo Cristofaro
(maternal grandparents) at the family Vinyard circa 1950

Vincenzo Prezio,
paternal grandfather
(notice the mustache!)

Anna Maria (age 12) and Mamma
in our living room

Family Portrait, Shortly After Arriving in the U.S.

Mamma on the patio, circa 1996

Anna Maria Prezio,
Director and District President,
Executive Entrepreneur Program

Roggiano Gravina, Provincia di Cosenza, 1949

Family home, Roggiano Gravina, circa 1950

Restored family home, 2004

PART TWO:

BASICS OF FENG SHUI AND GHOSTS

The following chapters consist of the basics of feng shui so you can better understand the connection I make between feng shui and ghost-busting. Chi, the life force and another name for energy, is also referred to as Qi or Ch'i, all having the same meaning.

Chapter 7: Art or Science

What about the scientific aspect of feng shui? The more I read about this subject, the more intrigued I became. The one fact that remains is that our modern day computer technology is based on zeros and ones. This system originated with the *I CHING.*

Also called the *Book of Changes,* it is the oldest of the Chinese classic texts. This ancient book consists of a series of symbols, rules for manipulating these symbols, poems and commentary. It is a binary sequential system and is the basis for the binary numeral system. Eventually, it was understood that the *I CHING* was the genesis for computer technology.

The reason feng shui is both an art and a science is that much of the time, as with doctors, having the knowledge and information is not enough. It's the implementation of the information that is defined as the art of feng shui. This multi-layered science, comes from what has been previously described as ancient formulas created by astronomers and understood by a few. In the Westernization of this technology, feng shui has either been diluted to what seems to be a simpler version of accumulated manuscripts, ancient books and translations. Some of it is even said to have been "lost" through the ages. What was handed down through masters and grandmasters was word-of-mouth or written down in such a form that today even the best translators cannot decipher.

Secrets of feng shui were purposefully written in their cultural dialect language code and even hidden in poetry. Only a few could translate it at that time. The few who were literate were considered doctors.

What we do know is that the emperors used feng shui masters to make way for conquests of territories. Wars were won through ancient techniques of feng shui. In some instances emperors would not allow the feng shui master in his house because they would have information that would affect the outcome. This was the test of his acumen. The feng shui master, if he knew what he was doing, would and should know these things just by observing the outside form and direction of the royal court and house. In some cases, if the feng shui master was unable to do his job, he was put to death.

Knowledge was privileged to only a few, who were handsomely rewarded for it and their ability to perform their duties. Women in those times were not permitted to be the Emperor's doctor, as they were called, or feng shui masters. They were also sworn to secrecy of what knowledge they did have. Women were forbidden to practice or even know any feng shui. If they were found out to practice, they were put to death.

Throughout history, the power of feng shui was kept from the common people of the land. It was forbidden to even 'know' these secrets. Hidden scrolls, word of mouth, changes written in code were mastered by a few.

The art of feng shui was translated in the 19th century by Christian missionaries in China. The missionaries called it "geomancy," which was a misnomer, since geomancy was then a method of divination that interpreted markings on the ground. In different countries geomancy takes the form of interpreting the topography of the land where location and landform is important and still accepted in many Asian societies. In the Western tradition, geomancy is based on the recognition of patterns.

Feng shui is not a religion, cult, superstition or magic. Traditional feng shui treats the environment as an integral element in the art of living. Proper application helps to balance the energy flow in our surroundings and create healthy and harmonious homes and buildings for maximum support of our personal and professional lives. Due to its power and effectiveness, feng shui was, for many years, a guarded secret, whose teachings were transmitted orally from master to student, and was not accessible to the general population.

The 20th century showed us how scientists better understood energy through two scientific theories. The Theory of Relativity by Albert Einstein, who understood that space and time were not separate but connected as space-time. And quantum physics by Niels Bohr, Max Planck and Werner Heisenberg, among others, which revealed that there is unity in all things.

Einstein understood feng shui principals and stood by it as a theory. He said, "Everything is determined by forces over which we have no control. It is determined for the insect, as well as for the star. Human beings, vegetables, or cosmic dust, we all dance to the mysterious tune, intoned in the distance by an invisible piper." This was posted in *The Saturday Evening Post,* October 26, 1929.

Today, feng shui is practiced by famous people like Donald Trump, Sting, Oprah Winfrey, Steven Spielberg, Richard Branson, as well as corporations like Coca-Cola, Sony, Shell, Procter & Gamble, Citibank, Disney, MGM Grand Hotel and Mirage Resorts, The Chopra Center, Creative Artists Agency and many others. They actively embrace feng shui because it adds value to their service, increases their profitability, and creates harmonious relations among employees.

Feng shui can enhance your business, promote teamwork, improve health, increase productivity, inspire your mind, increase prosperity and foster well-being.

Feng shui consultations can be performed long distance or through personal on site visits.

Chapter 8:
Earth Energy and Chi

The practice of feng shui is ancient, possibly 6,000 years old. Originally formulated in China to locate auspicious burial sites for the royal dead, feng shui made its way down from the Imperial palace, slowly, to the people. Much information was released with the intent to confuse, while the secrets of the feng shui masters remained carefully guarded. Over time, feng shui has evolved into a very complex and complicated science with many schools and masters. When asked how the various schools can all work, it is because feng shui is about moving Chi (Qi) energy, much like acupuncture.

In the world of feng shui, there are three kinds of Luck:

- Heaven luck, which is what we are born with,
- Man luck, which is what we do with ourselves and our lives, and
- Earth luck, our environment.

It is here, in Earth luck, that feng shui comes into play. The term "feng shui" translates as Wind and Water; Feng is the wind or chi, while Shui is water and fortune. Chi collects in water and is dispersed by wind. Feng shui is about harnessing the beneficial chi, or the universal life force, which permeates everything, and avoiding malevolent chi, which is usually man made.

When it moves like a gentle breeze, chi energy is positive. It becomes negative when it is allowed to stagnate. But when it is funneled too quickly along straight lines, it becomes actively harmful.

Chi is abundant around plants and forested areas; freshly cut flowers also attract it. Chi concentrates near running or bubbling water, especially waterfalls where the friction of water creates electromagnetic energy. Where chi is abundant, the oxygen level is also very high.

There are eight trigrams that form the 64 hexagrams of the *I CHING*. They are what formulate a pattern of movement. These changes or movements are used in the area of philosophy, astrology, Chinese medicine, numerology, martial arts, mathematics and feng shui. Feng shui is simply working with energy.

The eight trigrams are known as the Bagua. The Bagua represents yang or yin combinations, in stacked lines of sets of three. The trigrams are stacked from the bottom line up. The bottom line represents earth, the middle line represents man, and the top line represents heaven. The line that is different determines gender. The trigrams also represent the seasons, time of day, magnetic directions, five phases and corresponding colors, animals with human personality types, body parts,

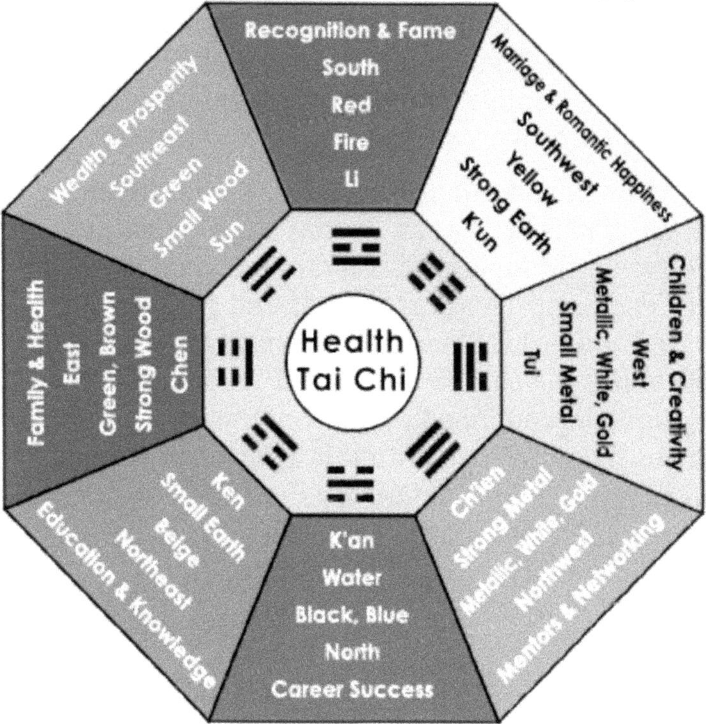

illnesses and numbers. They are also given a name depending on their energy, explaining their type of chi energy.

The male line is a solid yang and the female line is a broken yin line, each representing a position in the family hierarchy. There are eight members of the Bagua, just as there are in a family. The male members are father, oldest son, middle son and youngest son. The female members are mother, oldest daughter, middle daughter and youngest daughter. The Bagua is arranged in a pattern showing the configuration that includes all of these symbols, each one having a meaning.

The Bagua can also look like a grid. In feng shui the grid is used as an overlay map sometimes used over a floor plan. This method is used in Flying Star Feng Shui. This corresponds and correlates to the Luo shu or Lo Shu, also known as the magic square. It is the combination of all of the symbols and numbers contained in the configuration that gives us the outcome. With this information, a feng shui expert is able to determine the audit for the house or building. This is applied and implemented in any feng shui reading using the traditional methods.

Traditional or Classical Feng Shui

The Classical or Traditional Feng Shui Method used today uses the five elements and the physical setting of our environment. Using a Luo Pan or compass to determine direction, and the

Chinese mathematical system of calculating electromagnetic fields around us.

Developed in the Fukien province, China, it employs direction and the compass where the relationship of various elements in the Chinese universe – the stars, the *I CHING,* which stresses constant cyclical change, and others are charted in concentric circles around a compass. The feng shui originating in Kiangsi province, China, was

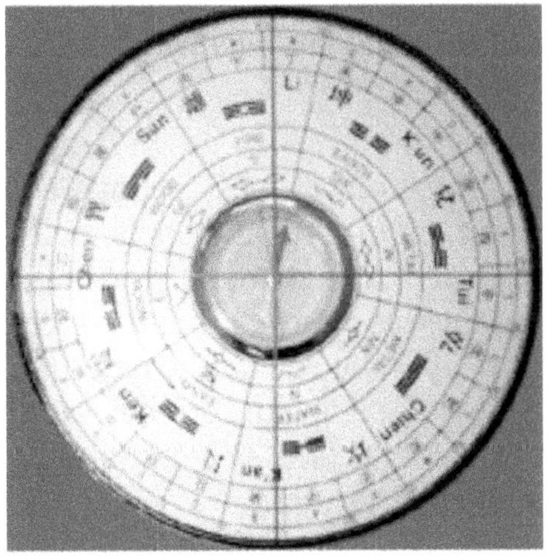

concerned with shapes and directions of land and water masses. This created what is known as Form School. Feng shui is also known by many as the art of geomancy.

Black Hat or Black Sect Feng Shui

Tibetan Trantric Black Hat Feng Shui is practiced by only a handful of experts. It's a hybrid of many customs, thoughts and practices. It came from Buddhism from India and through Tibet and finally to China. It incorporates religious rites and disciplines from the countries it passed through. It is riddled with magic, rituals, chants and charms. When it arrived in China, it was influenced by the yin-yang theory and Taoism. The outcome of Black Hat Feng Shui is an eclectic version based mostly on intuition and mystical knowledge.

Color

Color affects our moods, feelings, souls, culture, psyche, environment, beliefs, body parts, and feng shui time and placement. Historically, in ancient China it was believed that the forces of nature played a pivotal role in the determination of their luck and well-being, and so the uses and placement of color became very important to emperors as well as farmers.

Color became a major force in customs, cures and legends. Today scientific knowledge of color, nature and its effects on us are an integral aspect of our environment. Feng shui seeks to interweave the natural affects of color through placement, representative forms and relative time and harmonize our environment through the proper use of color.

Color can affect us, and stimulate us through various mediums such as paint, art, fabric, nature, and visualization.

Colors and Elemental Meaning

Red is fire element. It is not to be used to activate an area because of its vibrancy. A red colored object does emanate fire and the fire element. Fire element enhances and strengthens earth. There are earth energies that are the direct cause of sickness, arguments and accidents, so the fire element can increase or enhance these negative energies when placed wrongly. Be sure to place the red fire element in the right place because it can cause harm in the wrong location.

Red, to the Chinese culture is the most auspicious color, connoting happiness, power, warmth and strength.

White is the most fearsome color as it is the deepest color or lack of color. It is the color for mourning.

Earth is suited to the fire and wood element.

Fire is represented by the following colors and forms: reds, bright reds and any shade from the red spectrum, purple, bright lights, candles, lamps, up-lights, sun images, bright abstract art, triangles, pyramids, shapes of fire, fabrics representing fire, textures representing fire.

Earthy red tone colors will enhance creativity, fame and recognition.

Red or fire represents summer. Nurturing earth energy of the center sector will encourage health and harmony to flow. Red is worn by a Chinese bride. She wears a red or scarlet dress or cheongsam. Money is given in a red envelope because it is a very powerful color and said to multiply your gift if given in a red envelope. Purple is also an auspicious color. Worn by nobility, emperors, kings and high priests, it is considered high spectrum, high vibration, and high-energy color.

Blue is suited to water, wood and metal elements.

Water is represented by the following forms and colors: blues, black, deep purple, images of water, indoor water fountain, aquarium, wavy shapes, patterns and textures, even fabrics representing water forms and shapes.

Water placement and enhancements in feng shui is one of the most difficult of the formulaic calculations, so be sure to consult with a feng shui expert before placing this element.

Grey-blue colors will enhance spiritual and visionary quests. Its deep blue colors will enhance spiritual enlightenment and relaxation. Water can enhance career, communications and wealth.

White is suited to the metal and water elements.

Metal is represented by the following colors and forms: white, gold, silver, bronze, copper, stainless steel, metallic reflective finishes, coins, pendulum clock, bells, metallic ornaments and furniture, dome curved and spherical shapes and patterns. When placed correctly, metal can enhance creativity, health and productivity. White represents winter or a dormant state.

Green is suited for big wood and small wood elements.

Wood is represented by the following colors and forms: greenery, potted plants, a vase of freshly cut flowers, floral prints, columns, rectangular shapes, images of flowers and trees, tree of life symbols, bamboo, timber, cane, wicker furniture, vegetation, forests, woods and live plants of any kind. Green represents tranquility, growth, hope, freshness, health, family, wealth, and depending on the direction, spring (big wood) or late spring (small wood). Good healthy earth chi is the familiar emerald green.

Earth tones are suited for earth, stone and mountain elements.

Earth is represented by the following colors and forms: yellow, browns, earthy tones, mountain tones, mountain photographs, paintings or pictures, ochre, rock, ceramics, terra cotta, porcelain, earthenware, stoneware, statuary, quartz, crystals, gemstones, crystal sun catchers, crystal ball, square flat shapes and patterns, mountain patterns, cafe color, some orange colors, and beige tones and tans. These represent new success, strength, power, esteem, stability, knowledge, tolerance, wisdom, patience and experience.

Color and Meditation

Different colors affect your meditation. Green is considered the color of hope and recovery. White is for compassion. Red can be worn to ward off bad energies. In meditation, red can also expel negative chi. When visualizing color, your optic nerve is affected and this visualization influences our emotions thus causing a reaction to our health and wellbeing.

The Five Elements

The five elements relate to everything in the universe. They also relate to each other. When combined, they either harmonize and are productive, or they create a negative result. There are three cycles of the five elements; the productive cycle, the domination cycle and the reductive cycle. In feng shui it is crucial to balance out these five elements in your environment.

The domination cycle is sometimes referred to as the destructive cycle.

The Domination Cycle

Water extinguishes Fire

Fire melts Metal

Metal pierces Wood

Wood draws from the Earth

Earth blocks Water

You cannot destroy an element but you can change it. Therefore there is no such thing as a destructive cycle.

The productive cycle results when combined elements are harmonized thus resulting in good balance. This creates a beneficial result such as success, abundance, great health, good relationships, prosperity, creativity, and a great sense of balance and a feeling of well-being.

The Productive Cycle

Water helps Wood to thrive

Wood produces Fire when burned

Fire leaves Earth behind

Earth is the source of Metal

Metal liquefies into substance flowing like Water

In the domination cycle, the outcome is negative. The combination of these cycles can result in the opposite reaction and creates a clash in our lives. The imbalance can result in accidents, losses such as a job, financial problems, ill health, divorce, failed relationships, and a sense that nothing seems to flow in the right direction.

The reductive cycle is a draining energy cycle. This cycle is used by knowledgeable feng shui practitioners, who can balance energies by negating a certain aspect of too much energy drain in one area. It can be very useful to harmonize elements by draining the one that does not serve a purpose. This is in opposition of the productive cycle. Draining energy is a much more sophisticated way to remedy a specific environment.

The Reductive Cycle

Wood draws from water

Water corrodes Metal

Metal is formed in the Earth

Earth extinguishes Fire

Fire burns Wood

Draining entities and clashing energies are the primary focus when auditing an environment. Balancing the elements to create good feng shui is one of the ways to clear out bad energies. Once the elements are balanced and there is a clear path for healthy energies, it is impossible for negativity to thrive. Entities do not like high vibration and positive energy flow so it is easier to keep supernatural forces away.

Number Symbology

In feng shui, elements are represented by numbers. The numbers reflect a standard established through the *I CHING*.

Numbers correspond to a grid originating from the Lo Shu (see lo shu magic square), an ancient feng shui mathematical tool much like a grid. Each number represents an element:

Number	Element
1	water
2	soil
3	plants
4	plants
5	earth
6	metal
7	metal
8	earth
9	fire

Eight Aspirations

Directionally, the eight aspirations of life correspond to the compass direction.

You can find your compass direction by standing at your front door. With your back to the door, hold a compass in your hand and find out approximately what direction your door is facing. The facing also varies depending on the building's exposure and view. This is also called a bagua. It is octagonal in shape and also corresponds to compass degrees.

Compass Direction	Aspiration
Southeast	Wealth
South	Fame
Southwest	Relationships
East	Family and health
West	Children, creativity
Northeast	Education
North	Career
Northwest	Mentors, travel

You can place the bagua over your floor plan. It is used to understand the areas in your house and their designation. An example of the bagua's usefulness is knowing that if your wealth area is cluttered, you may want to clear it to allow for abundance and prosperity to manifest.

Evil Lines (Kong Wang)

Evil lines (Kong Wang) also called Void lines are compass, Luo Pan, directions that are to be avoided at all cost. The reason is that these areas of a house or building affect the occupants in a negative way. Symptoms are usually unexplainable. After moving into such a house or office, the residents begin to experience lack of drive or motivation, unemployment, stagnation, sickness, disturbances and arguments between family members. It often feels as if there is a negative energy that permeates the entire structure.

The 8 Evil or Void Lines are: 337.5, 22.5, 67.5, 112.5, 157.5, 202.5, 247.5, and 292.5 degrees. These are the intersection boundary of the 8 trigrams. If calculated, even plus or minus 3 degrees within the 8 void lines, these areas of degrees are to be avoided at all times.

Cardinal directions, North, South, East, West (0, 90, 180, 270 degrees) are better placement unless they fall within the void lines mentioned.

The Northeast direction is considered devil's gate. The Southwest is considered the devil's back door or "Dirty Temple." Spirits travel in a straight line. If the main door is facing Northeast, and the back door is sitting Southwest the home is considered to be unfortunate and can be easily haunted by spirits and ghosts. To remedy this, it is suggested that the Northeast door be slightly tilted. Spirits cannot negotiate turns at the angled door and would stop them from entering the house.

Structures in alignment with this configuration outside of the house or building can also have these same characteristics. In other words, if you were to draw a dotted line across from the void line to another structure that is behind the void line structure, you would get the same result. This is why it's called "evil line." During a compass reading, the compass can spin out of control. This is also an indication of the presence of supernatural beings or spirits.

Chapter 9: Remedies

In ancient times, observations about nature, climate, and the stars led the Chinese to the theories of Qi, Yin and Yang, and the Five Elements. This is the basis of feng shui and its roots are in Taoism, borne out of the shamanistic tradition that had existed in China for two thousand years. Attributed to a philosopher named Lao Tzu, also known as the Father of Taoism, who lived around 580 BC. He composed the Tao Te Ching (The Way and Its Power). Its philosophy was based on the natural order and harmony of nature. Tao, or The Way, taught that life should follow the creative path of nature and not that of human society.

The Taoist hierarchy never became as rigid as the Buddhists, while their association with magic and popular superstition endeared them to the people but lowered their reputation. The Taoists produced a vast pharmacopoeia. They investigated a multitude of properties, elements and plants in their pursuit of immortality; three emperors died within 30 years drinking Taoist elixirs.

Talismans, Amulets and Cures

While the use of talismans may be considered superstitious, feng shui, as a visual art, makes their use effective in boosting beneficial properties in a given situation. Feng shui enhancing tools are mainly used to regulate invisible energy and are secondary techniques. If a property is good, these tools are not necessary. But if the opposite is true, these tools will work up to a point.

Oftentimes there is a psychological impact of objects on an individual. This is why objects that depict warriors, bloody subjects, pain, torture and devils are not recommended as a feng shui remedy. These objects should be removed to engender peace and tranquility.

Rock Salt

Because of its absorbent nature, natural sea salt, rock salt or kosher salt are all useful for protection. I use rock salt to expel negative energies and ghost release. If a space feels odd to you, or the energy is uneven, or if you have had a fight, unwanted guests, or illness, try placing saucers of rock salt in each of the four corners of the rooms of the house. Leave it out for a few days then throw it away washing your hands after doing so. If you deal with the public, or are in business meetings, try keeping a red pouch of rock salt next to your heart to absorb any negativity that might be aimed your way. Keep a pouch in your purse and travel with some to counter the energy of strange hotel rooms. You can also put out saucers of rock salt in bathrooms to absorb their negative chi, but it must be replaced frequently. Another method is to put a bowl of uncooked rice on top of the toilet; since rice grows in water it will symbolically lift the Sha Chi of the toilet.

Rock salt is good to have around as it acts as a ghost deterrent. Place a tablespoon on both the left and right side of your front door. This will get rid of unwanted negative energies, especially strangers coming into your home.

Xiong Huang Wine

Realgar is arsenic sulfide, or shiung huang in Chinese. In Arabic it means "stuff from the mine." It was considered to be an elixir of immortality, however it is poisonous, so use it with care. Spiritually, realgar emphasizes the prophylactic power of sulfur. Realgar can be purchased in little packets at Buddhist shops in Chinatown. Its spirit chasing properties last for seven years after which time it must be re-applied.

To rid a property of unwanted energies or unsettled land spirits, mix realgar powder in a glass of wine, newly opened and purchased just for this, and place it as needed. This works well around a perimeter of a swimming pool, rocks that are too large and cannot be moved, or big trees that are blocking the chi from the house. Remove the liquid after at least 24 hours and pour it into the ground. Wash your hands before and after this method.

Cinnabar Powder

Cinnabar is sulfide of mercury and called Ju-Sha in Chinese, meaning literally red sand. It can also be purchased in small packets in Buddhist shops and is associated with power and protection. Mix it in a bowl with uncooked rice and nine drops of strong spirits (151 proof rum is preferred) and use it to bless a new property and dispel any evil spirits that may be lingering about. It is good for moving into a new home on the first day of your move.

Coins

While some Masters prefer the use of Chinese coins, which are round with square holes cut in the center, others use the coins of their particular country. When using coins the Yang or face side should always be up.

The Five Emperor Coins are the most commonly used; these come from the Qing Dynasty (1644-1911) considered the strongest and most glorious of all the Dynasties, as well as the last. Made of bronze, as well as some copper and silver, they were used and in touch with so many people that they are thought to carry a great deal of chi.

Qian-long was the famous emperor who ruled the strongest period of the last Chinese dynasty, Qianlong Dynasty, (AD 1736-1795).

On the coin is written in Chinese, the "currency of the Emperor Qian-wu." These coins are considered to have powers and promote prosperity. The Square center within and the round circle shape have been used since the 11th century BC.

In five elements, the square shape in the center is the earth energy and the circle is representative of heaven, so it nurtures metal. This is a productive cycle. The combination drives wealth luck. When energized, it brings in wealth and prosperity and drives out negative forces.

A Taoist ritual involves symbolically planting coins in all four corners of your house, inside and out and in the corners of each room except the bathroom. If your staircase comes down directly to the front door place 6 coins face up and cover them and the landing with a red carpet. In an air conditioned office try taping six coins face up in the air ducts; since the air coming in is generating chi, this is thought to help with cash flow.

Sword of Coins

The origin of the Sword of Coins lies in the configuration of the handle of the constellation of the Big Dipper. It is a powerful form of protection and can be hung up horizontally above an afflicted window or door, or behind a desk – never in front. If it is placed behind you, then the hilt should go up and the pointed end down toward the floor. This is thought to keep out unusual and confrontational spirits.

Crystals and Rocks

While some masters dispute the value of the following objects, I have found them to be effective in certain situations. Before setting them in place, cleanse your crystals in a solution of rock salt and water then place them in the sun to dry.

Crystals have the ability to transform energy. While mirrors reflect negative energy back onto itself, crystals collect yin energy and radiate yang energy, thus harmonizing a home or office.

There are various reasons to use crystals and some remedies require natural crystals while others use man made crystals; indeed faceted crystals hung near a window are an excellent way to relieve stagnant energy in a room while they bounce their colors and lights all over the walls. There is an inherent danger with crystals when hanging them in windows where there are curtains and fire hazard materials because as crystals heat from the sun they can cause fires.

Crystals are not often used by classical or traditional feng shui practitioners. Those who use crystals believe that hanging them in a hallway deflects Sha Qi, and between a stairway and the main entrance encourages better circulation of Sheng Qi energy. Crystals can be used as an earth element as well, and in some instances for water element remedies, but only in areas where they are required.

If your front door opens onto a dark or narrow space or a wall, mount a crystal sphere on a sconce on the wall or place it on a table with a light on it to lift the chi. There is usually a light fixture in the ceiling that can be replaced with a hanging crystal fixture. This also works in the bend of a long hallway.

A large obelisk-shaped natural crystal in the center of your home will help dissolve tensions caused by quarreling. Shine a light on it to activate its soothing power. Place a natural crystal sphere at a 45-degree angle from the front door – the place your eye first lands upon when entering the house – and shine a light on it. This is a wealth area and will help activate money luck.

Yellow citrine spheres, and spheres made of calcites, are excellent wealth energizers since they suggest the power of earth chi.

You can also position a round mirror with a metallic frame here to dissolve gossip or worries from the office following you home. Don't let the mirror reflect the front door.

Bury 3 diamond shaped crystals five feet from your front door in a pyramid shape pointing out to deflect a neighbor's roofline or a road coming at the property. This also works with bothersome neighbors.

If you wish to keep your partner at home more, tie a natural crystal or rock with red thread and attach it to the foot of the bed opposite the side he or she sleeps on. For harmony place a deep geode type crystal tied with red string under the bed where both your feet rest at night. The cavity should face upwards.

At your desk keep a crystal paperweight or sphere on the right hand side to aid in concentration. To generate growth, use green colored natural crystals that look like a mountain and place them either in the Southwest or Northeast, or behind you in the office. Rose quartz crystals that are smooth are good for relationships while amethyst is best used in pairs.

Crystals also can be used to represent the Five Elements: citrine for Earth, jasper for Fire, sodalite for Water, tiger's eye for Wood and gold and silver for Metal.

Crystals disperse chi in areas where clutter tends to accumulate.

Rocks and Stones

Rocks and stones act as collectors and controllers of chi. As earth elements, they carry similar energy as crystals do, except they are used to "ground" the energy, rather than uplift or transform it. A smooth, round stone is good for soothing jangled nerves as rocks have the ability to cool excessively hot chi.

For protective purposcs, a stone should be six inches or larger. If your stove is situated in the West or Northwest, or if it is metal clad, place two round rocks on either side of the back burners to help mitigate the clash of Metal and Firc. Largc round rocks can also be placed around a swimming pool to control the excessive yin nature of water too close to a house. If your house or property has a large stone on it that has been there for some time, it is the house's protector; leave it in place. If you must move it, move it to higher ground but don't get rid of it.

Sound and Light

Sound can be soothing, peaceful, calming and good for our bodies and soul. Quite the opposite is true when sound is noise pollution like traffic, sirens, construction work, loud arguments, screaming, screeching, and certain types of music. These are considered sound sha chi and create disharmony. Energy moves with sound and can stimulate areas that are yin. Sound changes vibration and moves energy from yin to yang. Use sound in a large area where there is little or no activity to ward off negative influences.

Light is similar to sound in that we can have too much or too little. Not enough or too much can hurt us in many ways. An example is a sunburn or sun poisoning. Light changes and stimulates energy. It moves and elevates chi. When light is placed properly it can change a yin or dark area to a light and yang place.

Bells

The sound of pleasant bells placed on a door handle is thought to help activate recognition; they are good for business as well as a home. You can also string eight coins along with the bells on a red string to bring more money into the household. Single bells blowing in the wind make a lovely sound and are often preferred to wind chimes.

Wind Chimes

Wind chimes are also useful to activate the chi of recognition, but they are to be used with caution as they can attract wandering spirits. Never use them inside a house; only use them outside. Avoid Ghost Gates; Northeast and Southwest areas. Five metal hollow rods are always good as they represent the Five Elements but listen to them first and make sure the sound is pleasing and not "clanking," a non-resonant sound.

Music

Although not true feng shui, the use of music can help lift chi in an excessively quiet house. It can help raise our vibration as well. If the house is large or has too many rooms for too few inhabitants, music will help to "fill" the space. The music should be pleasant and also works to keep the energy balanced if the inhabitants are away from the house for long periods of time. Music is a yang element.

Light

Lights belong to the element of fire and they too have their uses. Light can transform a yin place into yang. A small light left on most of the time can relieve a dark corner. Up lights in the corners of a sunken room can help lift the chi. Night lights left on in bathrooms can help to "burn up" some of the malign energy caused from all the water elements.

Lights in front of a house are good to promote recognition; never let a house get too dark.

Light in dark hallways and entrances can move chi along these paths creating better flow. Too dark or too quiet a place can invite spirit activity.

Chapter 10: Animals

In Taoist theory, nature is the most important aspect of life, and by living in harmony with it, man will prosper. The use of talismans is believed to be of help in connecting man with both the earth and the heavens. Some of the following animals are real and others are mythical. Their true affect is debatable. However, they add a psychological component of protection.

Mythical Animals

Dragons

Dragons are believed to live in the waters of the earth, as well as in the sky, and are considered to be very powerful. Dragon symbols, when placed next to water, are thought to bring prosperity. A dragon can be displayed next to the kitchen sink – if you keep your sink clean – to attract wealth, but do not do this at work, only at home and not if the kitchen sink faces a toilet.

Do not display dragons over a fireplace or use them as design motifs on rugs, nor should they ever be positioned under stairs. They should be kept out of bedrooms unless used to activate a particular remedy placed by a feng shui professional. Do not display a dragon in the Northwest, as this is the place of the Dog and dragons clash with dogs. A dragon symbol raised up on the upper left hand side of your desk will protect you. Place a dragon-headed turtle behind you and it will spare you from office politics. You can have more than one dragon image in your home; two, four, eight or nine but never five.

Dragon Tortoise

The Dragon tortoise is a powerful symbol of protection and can be placed behind you at work for support, or behind your house on a wall to stimulate a mountain. The Ho Tu numbers, as shown here, can also be taped underneath the Dragon Turtle to further protect you. Be sure his head faces the house.

Qi Lin

Qi lins are symbols of good fortune that bring peace and protection. They help guard the Tiger or female side of the house and should always face outward, back to back, the male on the left and the female on the right. You can use them on the right hand side of your desk to protect you at work. They can also be used against construction sites. If you live in a house where the orientation of the front door or the rooms are not auspicious for you, try

Ho Tu Numbers

7
2
8 3 5 4 9
1
6

writing down the Ho Tu numbers and displaying them alongside or underneath the Qi Lins.

Real Animals

Birds

In Taoists belief, birds, since they live in the air, are considered to be messengers of the cosmos and are as auspicious as fish.

The Phoenix, while not real, is thought to be the queen of all feathered creatures and will help you through hard times, bring turnaround success and new opportunities. Being a Yang symbol, place it high up when displayed and let it soar.

The magpie is considered to be a bird of joy; it is a good omen if spotted near your house and a picture of one or a pair will bring you much success as well as new friends into your life.

The crane is a bird of immortality and is identified with happiness and a long life. A pair of cranes signifies family harmony and well-being.

Ducks displayed in a pair symbolize married bliss. When carved out of semiprecious stone, they are at their highest potency, especially if they are made of jasper. These are best in the Southwest or Northeast corners of the home. While ducks symbolize conjugal fidelity, a pair of geese soaring high together signifies the happy togetherness of the married state and is especially useful if the couple in question each travel often on business.

Birds of prey signify wealth, while small birds, such as sparrows, indicate good news. Crows mean some divine message can be expected, perhaps in the form of a dream, while owls tell of a teacher of great significance coming into your life.

When selling your property it is auspicious to have bird symbols, pictures or paintings near your front door.

Horses

Horses represent success. A statue of a horse by your front door is thought to bring recognition and good fortune. Use one or eight horses; never use four or five. South is considered the best place for a horse, especially in an office. To sell a property, place a horse in motion. Ideally, all four feet should be touching the ground and they should be on a red cloth in each of the four corners facing the front door. Since the horse is considered a fire element, be careful not to place this fire element in areas not needing a fire remedy.

Rooster

Use a rooster to symbolically “eat” streetlights and electrical poles. The mouth should face the offensive part. Only use one rooster, as more than one will fight. Place a rooster on your desk at work to eat away at gossip and office politics. Do not use a rooster if you were born in a Rabbit Year; use mirrors instead. A rooster can also be used in the place of a Phoenix.

Snakes

The Snake is regarded as a Little Dragon and represents earth energy. Its place is coiled in the middle of every room and especially in the middle of the house where its round shape brings peace and protection to the household. Round rugs, round coffee tables, and rounded stacked or coiled objects are representative of the Snake.

It is interesting to note that the ancient Romans also considered the snake to be a protective, household deity.

Dogs

Dogs offer protection and also bring money. Fu dogs are better for a house as opposed to lions, which are considered to be too fierce. Dogs should always be displayed in pairs with the male on the left hand side of the front door looking out. It is best if they are made of ceramic and display them high up. Fu dogs can also be at the back of the house where they stand guard. If you are born in the year of the Dragon do not have statues of dogs.

Fish

The breeding of ornamental goldfish began in the Song Dynasty during the reign of Huizong (AD 1101-25). By the 16th Century it was a popular domestic pastime.

Fish represent abundance, joy and wealth. If you are having problems with co-workers, people in general, family members or neighbors, display a symbol of two fish kissing. This wards off negativity.

Zodiac Animals

The Asian Zodiac is comprised of twelve animals in a circle. By displaying these animals it is thought that people will be more supportive of your endeavors. Under your main phone, you can put a picture of the Zodiac Animals on top of a round mirror, which is on top of a red piece of cloth cut in a circle. This is a Black Hat technique thought to activate easy communications.

The Chinese astrological animal representations are:

Rat

1936, 1948, 1960, 1972, 1984, 1996, 2008

Ox

1937, 1949, 1961, 1973, 1985, 1997

Tiger

1938, 1950, 1962, 1974, 1986, 1998

Rabbit
1939, 1951, 1963, 1975, 1987, 1999

Dragon
1940, 1952, 1964, 1976, 1988, 2000

Snake
1941, 1953, 1965, 1977, 1989, 2001

Horse
1942, 1954, 1966, 1978, 1990, 2002

Sheep
1943, 1955, 1967, 1979, 1991, 2003

Monkey
1944, 1956, 1968, 1980, 1992, 2004

Rooster
1945, 1957, 1969, 1981, 1993, 2005

Dog
1946, 1958, 1970, 1982, 1994, 2006

Pig
1947, 1959, 1971, 1983, 1995, 2007

Deities

The God of Wealth

Statues of the God of Wealth, or Kai Guang, can be carved in wood, molded in clay or cast in bronze. In order for them to realize their potential, a ceremony should be performed by a Taoist priest to "open the eyes" of the deity. These can be placed on the #8 wealth star or the #9 future wealth star (Flying Star), or they can also face the front door or set in the peace corner of the house.

Kuan Yin

Kuan Yin, the Goddess of Mercy, is used to enhance the human aspect of the household. She is good in the sitting direction, not the facing. Besides using a Kuan Yin to bring good luck to the house, there are other items that can be used. Large viewing rocks, jade pyramids and eight sided pagodas can all help provide support when placed at the back of the property.

Kuan Yin represents loving, compassionate, serene and protective energy. She is believed to hear prayers and grants wishes of those who appeal to her for children, prosperity and harmonious families. Her birthday is the 19th day of the 2nd lunar month.

PART THREE:
GHOST-BUSTING

Chapter 11: Confused Entities

Ghosts, spirits, entities, souls and supernatural forces can move on to their realms and not force themselves to stay in a tormented state. They have a false sense of their own reality on earth and on our human plane. They belong elsewhere. As unseen energy, they do not need to be chained and shackled here. They need to break out of their imprisoned state, for they have no idea that they can be free to be in a better place.

For some unknown reasons they have not crossed over to their happier side and their misery creates disturbances with the living. They don't know that they are dead. They know they have powers to enter our reality, even though their powers are limited. The longer they stay in that state, the longer they will not want to leave this dimension. The longer they stay where they have gotten settled, the longer they will stay in that very same place.

If they are in a house where they lived when they were alive, they will not want to go to the other side. The entity is attached to its place where it spent most of its "alive" life. Certainly, this is disruptive to the living beings who have moved into that house. The new owners are disrupted and are constantly on edge about living in a place with a spirit. This creates an uneasiness and fear that makes them want to move out of their own house.

The spirit still believes that the house belongs to them and so tries to get rid of the new owners. How do they do this? They make noises during the night through door slamming, creaking of floors, banging and moving objects in the house and various other types of tones and noises that most definitely brings on fear to the real owners. Lights and fixtures turn on and off for no apparent reason. Shadows, a smoky or misty haze, and orbs show up in photos. Even the actual ghost or entity creates a form and shows up in the photograph.

The reality is that the entity is on a limbo plane. They want to stay here on earth but they don't know how to adapt. They have very limited powers to disrupt humans and their biggest challenge is to create these disruptions because of their limited abilities.

Ghosts are a metaphysical disturbance. Some really want to stay and some don't know what to do. They are confused about where they are and where they want to go and be.

Ghosts that are poltergeists can create great movement. They can come from someone who is alive. A teenager or someone who has pent up anger can activate it. Salt Water Remedy is a very good way to get rid of unwanted ghosts if they appear in an area that is conducive to entities and ghosts.

Every year there is a negative influence in a particular part of the building whether it's a house or an office building. The negative influences are in the Northeast and Southwest sectors. These two areas are known for the appearance of ghost activity. The reason is because northeast is call "ghost gate" in Chinese metaphysics and southwest is the most yin area of the Bagua. Southwest is the mother, feminine and yin, where the 3 yin Trigram resides. Ghosts, entities and spirits like yin places. This is why it is more common to find ghosts in these two directions.

Wind chimes can attract ghosts and entities. These objects do not belong inside a house for this reason. Any misplaced wind chimes on the outside can activate ghosts and create disruptions in those areas. Where there is ghost activity, it is important that the area remains light and very yang with sun, music, movement of some kind, and happy activities. Ghosts love yin spaces that are dark and damp, and dry and without activity.

Chapter 12: Feng Shui and Spirits

The Annual Feng Shui Flying Star is an indicator of either balance and harmony or disruptive imbalance and incorrect feng shui. Only a knowledgeable feng shui master consultant can determine this using their tools, such as a compass, formulas and feng shui principles.

One of the principles teaches us that that flow of life energy (chi) makes it possible to improve the quality of your life. Positioning a house, rooms and even surrounding land and gardens can affect our energy flow.

Flying star methods use formulas that incorporate time and space dimensions. It's important to know that the quality of the energy and the direction of the flow of chi changes with time and every 20-year period.

The changes can either be good or bad for us. It can improve our luck or cause havoc with our fortunes. The negative flying star is the number 5 star, also called Tragedy or Sickness star. It is also known as Wu kuei or "five ghosts or demons." It is an unlucky star.

Spaces, according to formulas, can have more than one type of star energy or multiples of the same star to them. Rooms that have one or two of this unlucky star in the skeletal structure calls upon ghost or entities. Depending on that formula, a feng shui master can harmonize the environment and bring about a calmer and more balanced house or office.

Even though feng shui practitioners use this technique by taking advantage of this ancient Chinese art, it is also important to note that dowsers, and practitioners who clear space are well versed on unseen energies. It is important to find a knowledgeable professional.

Each room has its own set of flying stars. It is not just the house or building's flying stars that determine the sequence outcome, but the annual flying star that is a concern, if its not creating an energetically correct balance of the elements within that space. If the space is so out-of-balance then things like foreign energies are attracted to this negative chi energy and will want to be a part of the stagnant chi.

Yes, ghosts hang out in stagnating negative energy. We can't see it, but it does exist. Suspending belief of reality that is seen can help in accepting the fact that there is unseen energy that exists all around us on a daily and perpetual basis. Electricity is one of them. Lightning is seen energy created by a force or collision of elements. No one insists on proof of electricity.

Chapter 13: Intense Energies

The clearing or extraction of entities via metaphysical means is performed by experts in the metaphysical profession. Sometimes a combination of clearing, feng shui methods and dowsing can get rid of the entity. Timing is of the essence because, as previously stated, they can either be so set in staying or are very willing and ready to cross over to a happier place – where they should have gone in the first place.

Practitioners often use a pendulum, salt water, incense, essential oils, candles, sage, prayer and compassion with the entity when asking them to leave. Asking the entity to relinquish this world and be released in a very gentle and kind way is often key to a positive result. Placing salt around the perimeter of the house or building and using persuasive gentle asking, as well as using a pendulum, to clear them are some of the ways practitioners can release ghosts. If there is more than one, sometimes one of them will leave and one will stay, so it takes perseverance and could take several tries to rid of the stubborn ones.

The energy it takes to do the clearing and feng shui is intense. Protection and precautions are not necessary if we come from a place of love, and with the spirit of helping others. This protects us and is recognized by energies, entities and spirit beings. Having said that, I do wear red and protective oils as well as rock salt, which deters unwanted entities.

Wearing oil or red raises your vibration. Sage burning is optional and gets attention, but is not absolutely necessary. The intention of clearing out any unwanted spirits or entities is easier if the approach is friendly. They are not usually evil but are more lost and do not know that they belong elsewhere. In addition to oil essence and red colors, fluoride is a protective semi-precious stone that deters electromagnetic energies.

Clearing is usually done room by room with prayers directed at the entity. It is the clearing that drives out and drives away spirits or entities. In actuality, clearing frees them and releases them from their negative lingering in a place and time where they do not belong. They are then liberated to the appropriate dimension of their time and space, as well as their own energy comfort zone where they will find the peace and comfort that they crave.

You can attempt to do this. It's a tough and strange job that can be done. If you either don't want to attempt this or you want an expert Chi Buster, you can hire someone like myself. It could take time. It could take up to 3 or 4 hours. One of my ghost releases took me more than 3 hours. This is because certain feng shui methods were employed in addition to the ghost busting. Feng shui allows you to harmonize your environment through the implementation of elements that negate negative chi. Once this is done internally and externally, the stagnant chi energy is negated and only positive energy will survive in a correct feng shui environment. Not only does this technique remove stagnation, but also it increases negative ions so that the residents can be more productive and creative in all aspects of life. They will feel a sense of well-being.

More than one method is often employed to create a harmonized environment. Some of the methods used are space clearing, dowsing, feng shui, and enhancements, along with the chi busting methods.

The Central Palace, or center of the house or building, is the area to consider placing remedies. The reason for this is in the instances where the ghosts or entities are so strong and it is not known what part of the house or building they reside, the center of the house, also called the Tai Chi, is a collective and central aspect of the house. The Center of the house can be found by drawing an X from one extreme corner of he house to the opposite corner from all four corners. This is best accomplished on the floor plan.

Chapter 14: Space Clearing

There are two types of disturbances: metaphysical disturbances and earth disturbances. Dowsing is one space clearing method. Dowsing Rod and Pendulum are used to dowse a house. Certain questions are asked along the way by the dowsing or clearing expert to clear and balance an environment.

The question to ask: is the chi clear and balanced? Is there a primary cause of disturbance? Is the yin/yang balanced?

60 percent Yang is preferable. A dowsing rod is used to go through the environment, room-by-room to look for disturbances. As you go along, you would ask the same questions about the disturbances and whether or not they are metaphysical. The answers become clear.

Metaphysical disturbances are the unseen disturbances that come from people that live or have lived in the space. These disturbances can come from the land before any building was present. Some examples of these are negative thought forms of the current or previous occupant, such as fear, anger or emotional trauma. Ghosts, poltergeists, or disturbed spirits of the land (can come from home being built over a burial site) are also metaphysical disturbances.

Earth disturbances are those that can be from faulting pressure, underground water, excessive electromagnetic frequencies from inside the earth or man-made – like technology, transformers, high voltage electrical lines. Once disturbances have been identified, clearing brings balance to whatever disturbances are in the space.

Balancing the Yin/Yang energies, once identified, can bring harmony to the space. Most people do better within a 60 percent Yang energy balance. Too Yang can cause hypertension and over activity, while too Yin can cause depression. Remember that yin spaces are darker and quite inactive without much light and yang spaces have lots of light and activity.

Following chi flow from the entrance throughout the space of the building or house and throughout the entire property, allows the consultant to measure the negative or positive fields. After these areas are identified, clearing and shielding can begin.

Metaphysical disturbances, as well as emotional trauma, can be from previous owners, and not necessarily from present owners. Sudden violent death or acts of violence can be detected and cleared by a good metaphysician, who can actually sense, feel and even have physical symptoms of fatigue and tiredness while clearing the space they are in. Oftentimes these symptoms are so overwhelming that a break is in order. Some other symptoms can be sneezing, watery eyes, runny nose, which is an indication of an 'inner crying' from someone who once lived or is living on the property. Deep emotional turmoil, pain or sorrow can also be felt from current or previous owners. Loneliness, despair and even smells and senses of alcoholic entities can be felt. Eye twitches are fear issues from present and previous occupants.

Ghosts can show up in any room at any given time. They must be cleared quickly. This will make it easier to clear the rest of the house. Retracing a path to eliminate any other ghostly disturbances is also done to make sure that there is no residual affect from the previous clearing.

A report can help to clarify and show all entities and energies that come up during dowsing. These can be vibrational frequency imbalance, dark forces, pollutants from the land, such as fertilizer or something buried in the land.

Clutter

Clutter is litter, disorder, chaos, rubbish, confusion and disarray. Clutter clogs energy and keeps chi from flowing properly. It is impossible to find things with clutter. Clutter is unnecessary and adds to confusion. It keeps us from getting what we want and need in life. It pollutes our mind and thoughts. It is, by far, the single most offensive culprit that does not allow healthy energy to circulate in the environment. It keeps us stagnant emotionally, physically and mentally. It creates harmful stagnating chi.

What we do not need or use, we should give away and let someone that needs it use it, or we should throw it away. Detaching and letting go of things is a good way to allow new opportunities to manifest in our lives.

My formula for discarding what you don't really want or need is this: Ask yourself this question when going through the material you are trying to clear, "Does this make me feel happy or sad?" If it evokes a negative feeling, then you don't need it. Let it go.

Chapter 15: Earthly Disturbances

Earthly Disturbances occur from non-metaphysical sources and are material, man-made for the most part.

Faulting pressure, whether located in the substructure or walls, can contribute to disturbance. This pressure must be released.

A Tibetan singing bowl over the space(s) is used at the end of a clearing to sanctify and further clear any negative disturbances. The vibrational resonance from the sound has a powerful healing influence.

Asking the discerning energy field to be placed around the environment whether it is a home or office, filters out negative influences that are not for the client's highest good.

Clashing chi occurs when the negative and stagnant chi energies are removed and healthy chi replaces negative chi. This clash manifests in electromagnetic charges. Some of these charges will cause electrical equipment to stop or light bulbs to actually pop. This is good news, although at the time it appears disturbing. I have seen clocks stop, clock hands turn in the opposite direction; cell phones give out crazy messages and telephone numbers and even entire electrical systems shut down. It's not an unusual phenomenon.

Too much electromagnetic energy inside and outside of a house often causes disease, ill health and a malaise for the residents. Symptoms include poor concentration, irritability, sleeplessness, tiredness and many others. The electric charges can be so powerful that remedies are a necessity. If your house is very close to electric sources such as transformers, power lines and power sources, this could also be the source of disturbance and poor health.

Chapter 16: Feng Shui Experts - Yin and Yang

Feng shui consultations, audits and readings on environments such as homes, businesses and preconstruction sites are usually for the purpose of correcting the environment so that it assists the occupants or owners with relationships, health issues, disruptions or money problems. Upon entering a home, a good feng shui consultant can assess quickly whether or not the environment is inviting.

After a brief assessment, the client becomes familiar with the consultant and can usually articulate that there is some disturbance in the house. Some clients know what it is and some don't. Feng shui is powerful in that it can align a misaligned space. It can cause an imbalance or a balance and it can harmonize or cause disharmony among its occupants.

If the owners are not feeling a sense of peace or well-being, and they feel that their lives need improvement, they call a feng shui expert to help them remedy their environment. Feng shui can correctly identify and adjust these imbalances. Yin and Yang energy in a home or office can cause some types of homes to be more susceptible to entities such as ghosts.

Yin energy invites the presence of entities. Usually, the compass needle vibrates or spins if there is ghostly energy present. This can occur even if the house is within close proximity of a Yin area such as a cemetery, church and even close to a hospital.

Yin energy is feminine, dark, receptive, still, cool, quiet, inactive, stuffy, damp. Yin energy is reserved for supernatural energies, cemeteries, burial grounds, gravesites, mausoleums, churches, and graves. A yin zhai is a home for the dead.

Yang energy is male, active, moving, light, warm, bright, loud, lively, airy, cheerful. Yang energy is good for houses and offices full of people, occupants, residents and workers. A yang zhai is a living person's home.

If you watch a child interact, you will notice that they choose to go to places where they feel a strong energy. Whether this energy is yin or yang, they are attracted to it. They like to linger in yang energy and are fearless of yin energies, for the most part, but will want to leave any negative influences unless the entity "captures" their interest.

Animals, such as cats or any type of feline, will want to stay in negative energy and are attracted to yin energy and entities such as ghosts. They often "know" in advance if someone is about to pass on, and appear to comfort them or help them move on. They see ghost and sense them.

A friend was telling me the story of her cat who was scratching her left breast constantly. She said that this had never happened before and was getting annoyed at her cat. I told her to see her doctor and to have her doctor order a mammogram. The results of her test were positive – they found breast cancer in her left breast in its early stages. The good news is that the cancer was removed and she is cancer free. That is not to say that all cats are able to detect or should be used as a detective device, but she was able to notice her cat's behavior as irregular and abnormal. Along with my knowledge and recommendation, she was able to go see a doctor in time to catch the disease early.

A dog is different. Dogs are yang, unlike cats, who have a yin nature. Dogs like to be in very active and moving places. They help to shield, secure and guard their owners. Their nature is to be loyal and protective, but in a different way than cats. Some dogs can hear entities and some can see ghosts, but they are not driven like cats to be with them or go in search of them. Quite the contrary, dogs want to get rid of them.

Chapter 17: Yin Houses

 house located in close proximity to a cemetery or a church is a yin house.

Although a church is a place of worship and peace, it is yin because one goes there to pray and to worship. It is also a place where people are laid to rest or attend funerals and pray for the dead. Even though happy occasions, such as weddings and baptisms, oftentimes take place in a church, it is a place where people pray to their God, saints, their deceased family members and friends, angels and other spirits.

Hospitals, nursing homes, sanitariums, insane asylums or mental hospitals and recovery houses are also yin places where people die or are in pain and discomfort. Houses near hospitals are also said to be in too yin a location. Houses built near these buildings are affected by their energy.

A house near or over a burial site or sacred ground, or where there may have been a ceremonial site, is also yin space.

A building or house where someone living in it died, whether suddenly or violently, such as battlefields, jails, war prisons, or the occupant died of a disease are yin places.

Houses where there are weeping willow trees or a banana tree on a property are yin places, especially if these trees are in close proximity to the house.

Houses that are too dark inside with trees surrounding the building not allowing sunlight inside are yin.

Houses with not enough windows to allow light inside are yin.

Houses that are decaying and in a declining cycle, where the life energy of the house is no longer, can attract entities.

Houses that are newly constructed can have ghosts as well, if they were built on sacred grounds or burial grounds or where there has been a battle or war where people have died. These are also considered yin places.

Houses containing wind chimes or bells inside that are not placed correctly also attract ghosts. Feng shui placement of chimes is usually recommended for the exterior of houses and must be placed in a certain direction.

Houses that are not well lit, and the sun rarely shines in through windows, are yin spaces where ghostly entities could be living.

Houses built into the side of a mountain are considered to be too yin.

Houses where past owners or occupants were very attached to the house and property, even though they have passed away, are yin.

The life energy of the house that is in the cycle called Si or Shuai is weaker than a house that is prosperous or Wang, or in their Sheng cycle.

The main entrance of a house is the most important aspect in feng shui, as it is considered the mouth of the house where chi comes into the house and is distributed through out the house. Every time the front door is opened new chi enters. Good energy comes in when the front door is positioned properly, as determined by feng shui compass directions. When the entrance has stagnant chi entering, then it becomes too yin and not prosperous.

Entrances of a house should be well lit, bright, airy and fresh. A dark entrance does not allow for renewed energy to enter.

Pathways to entrances and doorways should be curvy and meandering, right up to the door. Garden paths and borders should also adhere to the same configuration rather than sharp, pointy geometric designs. Spirits and entities travel in straight lines and do not go around bended and curved pathways.

When the entrance of a house is in a flying star 5, according to feng shui calculations, there is sickness and yin energy at the front door, which will not help to support good energy. It will attract ghostly energy and illness. This number 5 brings problems wherever it resides in the house and must be remedied, otherwise it will attract unwanted entities and obstacles.

Houses with negative energy have what I call a 'fear feeling' to them coming from the stagnant negative energies and thus gives the person entering, if they really tune into the house energies, an "unsettled feeling".

Your front door is the "mouth" of the house or building. It is the gatekeeper for any and all chi coming in and going out. Just like our bodies, whatever we feed them results in how our bodies will respond. If we feed our bodies junk food, we will experience lethargy, low energy, poor health. The same is true with our homes. The energy should be clean, fresh, and not surging or fast moving into our entryway, the mouth of the house. Indoor and outdoor energies should flow in gracefully and not be ferociously forced into the structure. Slow down the flow of energy racing through by hanging mirrors and alternating them. So, don't hang them in succession. A rounded carpet or rug on the floor will also slow down energy. What you bring in should nurture your mind, body and spirit.

The front door is also an important aspect in feng shui. It should be solid, although it can have small windowpanes, particularly if the entryway is dark. The entry area should be well lit and appealing to the senses, and not cluttered or obstructed. The door should open with ease and the lock should be fixed if broken or uneasy to unlock. Keep this area clean and inviting.

The entry to any home remains the first impression. It is the same as meeting someone for the first time. First impressions are lasting impressions.

The Yin and Yang Areas of a House

The front of the house, which usually faces the street, is the Yang side. It also has the best view. The public rooms – the living and dining room – should be sited here, while the private rooms, the bedrooms, bathrooms and kitchen, should be located in the back or Yin side of the property, behind the central line.

Ideally, the front door should be in the front of the house, not on the side, and there should be windows looking out onto the street. Windows are the eyes of a house, if there are no windows visible from the front door then life will pass you by.

A large body of water behind a house is a very Yin feature. One of the problems with a swimming pool directly behind a house, or a property with a view, is that the floor plan is often turned around with the public rooms sited toward the pool or view, while the private rooms are located in the front. This shift often leads to confusion, as the occupants of the house no longer feel protected.

An even shaped house is always preferred to an odd shape. An L-shaped house by its very nature has a missing area and is considered to be a lonely house. A U-shaped house is even worse, depending on which area the U is located in. If it is in the front, it is like a person with no face. If it is in the back, the house lacks a backbone and the occupants will not be supported in life. The best thing to do with a U shape its to enclose it.

Always check for power poles, triangular shaped rooflines, corners of opposite buildings, and/or a large tree directly in front of the door. The front door should be easy to see and there should be windows looking out onto the street.

As a general rule, traditional houses have better feng shui form than non-traditional ones. Houses with good feng shui are often rectangular or square houses. Architectural surprises are not considered to be balanced, while walls of glass offer no support. Energy needs to flow evenly without sharp corners and multi-level rooms. Good chi cannot travel evenly. This causes disruptions and lack of balance in energy flow.

Even shaped property is a most important aspect. A square or a rectangular shaped house that is well "sitcd" is best. This means an armchair-like formation, secure, protected without any obstructions aimed at the front door or the windows. The public rooms should be located in the front and the private in the back. Big is not necessarily better; rather it is the flow of energy throughout the house that makes for good feng shui.

Staircases should not come directly to the front door; stairs are virtual waterfalls and water is money. If the stairs aim directly at the front door, money will pour out of the house. Some houses with this feature can be remedied by employing an experienced Feng shui consultant to implement remedies. It's a good idea to hire a feng shui consultant who can help you choose a house before you chase after an inauspicious one.

Chapter 18: Cultural Traditions and Beliefs

There are many traditions, beliefs, folklore, superstitions and myths regarding ghosts, shape-shifters, spirits, fairies, witches, entities, bogeyman, even cultural beliefs surrounding the existence of saints, angels and devils handed down through generations. Some stories such as miracles are taught in schools as true stories and not just simple myths or folklore. Some believe that are those who are empowered to bring a great curse upon a person. Most of these beliefs are fear based. These beliefs and traditions originate from different parts of the world.

In the Chinese culture, ancestors are revered, and as such there's a great deal of effort in pleasing them to increase one's prosperity and luck. It is believed that this creates good will with them and can influence their ability to help the living receive rewards such as winnings, good fortune, benevolence and even academic rewards.

The Chinese celebrate Hungry Ghost Festival, also known as the Qingming Festival. In traditional Chinese, the meaning is clear and bright. During this time, on the 14th night of the 7th lunar month

(August and some of the beginning of September), when ghosts are allowed to come through hell gate and the deceased visit the living, the Chinese pray to their ancestors and hold a large party to please them. The three realms of heaven, hell and the living are open and the Taoists and Buddhists perform rituals to transmute and absolve the sufferings of the deceased.

Ghost Month is a time of ancestor worship. The family of the deceased treats them as if they are still living. It is believed that their presence is felt and there is a strong chance of seeing ghosts. The living burn incense, give concerts, and make specialty items, such as paper money and products of all types, just for this occasion, to make the dead feel appreciated. Other than this festival, they are left undisturbed.

These ghosts, entities, spirits, fairies, and even ancestors, are respected and revered by not only the Chinese culture, but in other cultures as well. The Ghost Festival shares similarities with the Mexican observance of Los Dias de los Muertos (The Days of the Dead). Ghost Festival, with its theme of spirits and ghosts, is also known as the Chinese Halloween.

In the Irish culture, spirits even act as messengers. They understand the known and sometimes the unknown. There is a common thread among cultures in the belief of an underworld, and their respect for ghosts and the like. These cultures are influenced by the dead, and they try to preserve the traditions and beliefs of such powerful entities through the ages. Many cultures share these same beliefs although they may be called by another name.

Ghosts like to take shape and form. Items in a house that can be used by entities are portraits of ancestors, masks, even mannequins, if there are entities in a very yin house, otherwise, it is useful to know that if the house is very yang there is no need to remove these items.

We're all intrigued, fascinated and puzzled by ghosts. Movies are taken from real accounts, such as Poltergeist, The Amityville Horror and other ghost haunting stories. More and more ghost stories are being told and more books are being written about ghost stories, ghostly houses and encounters with entities.

Is there a way to get rid of ghosts and disturbances caused by entities?

Harmonizing a house with more yang energy and removing yin aspects of a house usually rids the house of entities and ghosts. Ghosts will leave on their own accord if asked to leave. This can be done in various ways. Feng shui remedies are used in combination with calling in a ghost or talking with a ghost.

Feng shui, clearing, dowsing, remedies, banging on drums, sage, salt, fire, candles, algar in wine, salt water lamps, compass calculations, opening certain passageways and doors, elements and various combinations of these methods can release a ghost or entity to go and live in its proper place and time. Some entities are stronger than others, and some are cunning and return after moving to another temporary location.

Chapter 19: Five Ghosts Carry Money

Some feng shui practitioners use a method called Five Ghosts Carry Money. This principal of feng shui is a specialized remedy that uses knowledge of how to use time, space, location and direction to turn a house that is negatively flowing with tragic outcomes into a house that has a profound turn-around with luck. It is a theory to be used by experts who know this guarded feng shui secret method.

In ancient times, this technique was passed on to sons and not daughters in the family and was used to help the poor and helpless. The reason why males were privileged in this case is that they may get hurt by the ghosts themselves and they did not want the females dealing with entities that might retaliate. It is called Five Ghosts Carry Money because it was once believed that ghosts and spirits affect this change to solve problems that then seemed like miracles. Even today, some teachers will claim this to be true.

This method comes from the ancient word of mouth techniques. This theory is often explained as a water method. Since water is the strongest of all the elements, using any water method takes expertise.

When this method is used properly, it can have profound changes in the dynamic flow of energy that is sometimes short lived. In this instance ghosts, entities and unknown energies can be very useful and often produce positive outcomes.

Taking the facing direction of the property and, if it is possible, the feng shui expert will place a water feature in the appropriate directions, along with the location of doors and windows that are also positioned and in the appropriate direction. If done correctly within the direction, time, and space, then Five Ghosts will bring the household money successfully.

Water is the most potent element. When you move into a house and there are lots of leaks, lots of water, pipes bursting often, electricity going out; it's a sure sign that there are ghosts in the house. If you walk into a place and you feel strange, listen to your intuition.

Chapter 20: Ghostly Houses and Feng Shui

The following stories are of actual places and real client houses where I was called in to clear out the presence of disturbing spirits. These are actual accounts of the people and remedies I employed to release these unfortunate ghosts. Some were more stubborn than others, and took more time to clear.

Walter

The first property is a house that was owned by an architect who died in it after a long illness. My client was reticent to tell anyone about a troublesome ghost, but she finally called me. It took time because the disturbing elements were bothering her and not her roommate. She could hear the noises and feel his presence but could not see him. Her neighbors and her roommate could see the ghost and were not bothered by him. Finally, my client's roommate gave her permission to call me in to release the entity.

When the ghost is welcome in the house, it is much more difficult to release it. The ghost seems more at ease having a willing tenant living in his space. This allows the ghost to carry on and continue to inhabit the house.

When alive, Walter had taken very good care of his house. The house had been remodeled. Rooms were added and spaces were extended, patios and terraces were enhanced and slanted ceilings were common in the living areas of the house. Walter, the previous owner, had occupied the house for almost his entire lifetime, until his death a little over a year ago. My client purchased the house from the family estate.

My client called me because there were disturbances in her house from the presence of a ghost. She heard disruptive loud noises, particularly in her bedroom. She never actually saw it, but the ghost was seen often by one of the occupants on a regular basis. Even the neighbors saw Walter on the rooftop hammering away in his favorite overalls. They saw him atop her bedroom area and the garage area where he had worked on many projects. They described him to a T because they had personally known him. They also knew his daughter, who sold the house to my client. Although she never saw him, my client could hear Walter banging away at night on the roof, and sometimes doors would slam. As she described it, weird noises would keep her up. My client had lived in the house for a year when she called me. She wanted relief from the unwelcome Walter.

Her roommate was out of town on the day I went to feng shui and clear the house. If he had been there, there may have been an incident complicating the release. As it was, Walter did not want me there.

How did I know this?

Soon after the clearing in the bedroom, I was in the family room and gathering my thoughts to move on to the next detail, when I felt a very strong weight pushing against my right shoulder and neck area. I froze still and waited for what seemed a long time, but was only seconds.

I looked across the room and my client was talking to my cameraman. Both of them looked at me and said, "What's the matter?" They knew something was off, because they saw my facial expression. Seconds after that, the pressure that had started to become painful ceased. I asked Walter to stop. I felt immediate relief. Even thought I did not see Walter, I felt his presence and knew he was trying to sabotage my efforts. When the photographs came back there were orbs and faint ghostly outlines in the pictures. Walter had to let go and he eventually did.

The front of the house was not too sunny, but the rear of the house, which is sitting West, was sunny and bright with landscaped architectural gardens and trees. A tall fence surrounds the house on all sides.

The left side of the house had very little support. By that, I mean that the left side (being the tiger side) was not balanced, since the front door was to the far left of the house. This is the tiger side or the feminine side. If out of balance, it does not support the female occupant. There are remedies for this issue but I understood why males dominated her house. She was not being heard.

Walter died in the bedroom, and the house had never been cleared or dowsed afterward. His wife had also died two years prior, but not in the house. My client could not sleep, was restless from the sounds, and wanted relief from this strange series of what had become common occurrences. The house was not particularly warm and inviting when I walked in. It needed a vibrational energy lift. Even though the house was not in a decline cycle, it felt heavy upon entering. Every 20 years a house goes through one cycle. This is also called the construction cycle. Remodeling can change the house cycles and this house had been updated. This created a new cycle and therefore the house was not in a decline cycle.

The disturbances were mostly coming from the northeast direction, and on occasion the southeast direction. The pattern of noise was directly related to the master bedroom where my client slept in the northeast sector of the house. This sector had yin energy and is also called Ghost Gate. The southwest sector also had the presence of the same ghost. The southwest is also considered the "backdoor" of evil forces, since it is the opposite direction of the northeast. This sector is the KEN trigram 8, which is considered the youngest son in the *I CHING* and is the "weakest" of the trigrams. It is therefore considered vulnerable to "evil influences." This is the reason it is called Ghost Gate.

After calculating compass directions and flying star, what I sensed was made even clearer. I used a Luo Pan compass. The needle was spinning out of control, a sure sign of disruptive energies. This indicates the presence of ghosts. The answer was clear. These sectors were yin with 5 Stars negative influences in the sectors mentioned. A vibrational lift was necessary.

Lighting these areas was key. After several feng shui remedies were installed as recommended, there were no more complaints about Walter. It seems simple, but it took several hours to clear the ghost out of the house in addition to the feng shui remedy implementations. My client was able to sleep soundly without disturbances immediately.

This house is located in Sherman Oaks, Calif., a respectable, middle-class suburb of Los Angeles. It was not necessarily dark, dingy, old, run-down, unattractive, secluded, eerie, cold or scary. It wasn't even cluttered or dreary. It was tastefully decorated, clean, well cared for, with ample open spaces, windows and light coming in. Large glass sliding doors allowed for breezy entryways. The house was only partially yin. This house was not near a cemetery or burial ground. It was not close to a church or house of worship.

The bedroom, and the entrance area, however, did contain a double five flying star or, as previously mentioned, two unlucky stars, which attract ghosts, entities and spirits. In addition, the house, on both sides, had neighboring swimming pools, both yin water elements.

During a feng shui consultation, I take photographs. This allows me to see things after the audit that I include in my report. There are objects that show up in photographs that ordinarily cannot be seen. They are called orbs. Orbs are circular anomalies appearing in photography and video. In size, they can be as large as a basketball and as small as a golf ball. Sometimes they leave a streak or tail if they are in motion. Orbs are both thought of as dust particles or moisture, as well as paranormal in nature. Some people even think that orbs are aliens monitoring us from outer space. However, the images observed by those who study them, are associated with supernatural activity and haunted places having odd shapes at times.

An orb is clearly showing in one of the photographs taken of the area where Walter used to sit in his favorite chair, which was left behind and sold with the house along with other items. Favorite items such as furnishings can also carry and absorb energies from previous owners. It's not surprising that the orb was seen around his favorite chair.

The day after the clearing I received a call from my client. I could hear a happy and relieved tone in her voice. She said, "Walter is gone. Thank you."

Carla

Carla's mother was very concerned about her daughter's dropping grades, poor sleeping pattern, stomach upsets and general malaise.

Carla was doing so poorly at school that her mother thought she might have to go to summer school. Carla is a very good natured, intelligent young woman. But she was also getting into angry arguments with her mother. Her mother had no idea how to handle all these drastic changes. Carla admitted to me that she saw a ghost in her house. Her mother knew about this entity and called me for help.

This family of three lived in a small house in Los Angeles. Carla was 16 years old at the time. She had not slept for long periods of time. In addition to this, she was having stomach problems and skin break-outs. Her mother and father were very concerned and had their family doctor order tests, such as ultrasound, blood tests, and various allergy tests. All of the test results were within normal range. Her mother called me, exasperated and wanting help. She knew that something was wrong.

During my interview with Carla, she admitted to me that she had seen a ghost repeatedly and this was troubling her. She was experiencing various sightings, noises, and unexplained disturbances. The most disturbing to her was seeing the shadow of a man in her doorway on many occasions.

It was not easy for Carla to talk about the ghost she had seen. I could sense her fear. She told me that she would close the door and the door would open again on its own. She would open the door and it would slam shut on its own. She heard noises and conversations when there was no one around and sometimes she would see movement of shadows. She even heard noises and conversations outside her window where there was no way anyone could ever be there, considering where the window was located in the rear of the gated house and on the ground floor. There were steps going down into her bedroom and she often heard the sounds of feet going up and down these steps. She heard walking up and down the steps to her front door as well. The most frightening of all, was her ability to recognize that it was indeed a male figure standing in her doorway who would not leave when she asked him to leave. All of these occurrences were causing her stress and dis-ease.

The previous occupants told Carla's family that they, too, had similar experiences with similar frequency. They also saw the figure of a man standing in the doorway in the same way that Carla had experienced it. The chatter would get louder and louder even after asking this spirit to stop. As time moved on, the noises were more frequent, louder and so disturbing, they caused them to move out after living in the house for five years.

I sensed that someone had died in the house. It was a young male who died in the house from a long-term illness. He was a smoker. The cigarette smoke permeated throughout the house, even though no one in Carla's family smoked, nor did the

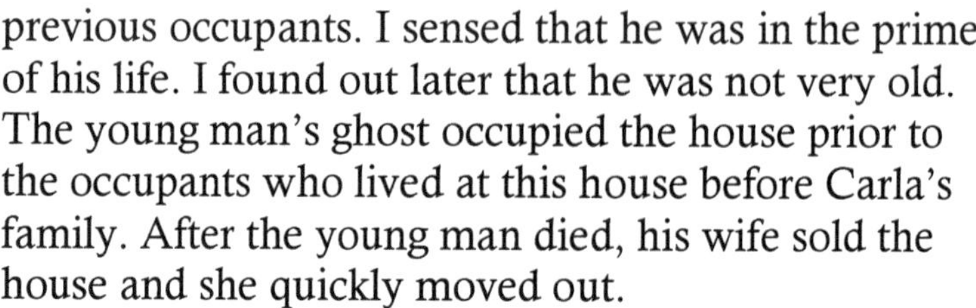

previous occupants. I sensed that he was in the prime of his life. I found out later that he was not very old. The young man's ghost occupied the house prior to the occupants who lived at this house before Carla's family. After the young man died, his wife sold the house and she quickly moved out.

I was called in almost five years to the day that Carla's family moved in. The disturbances had caused arguments, financial loss, legal battles and even stalking by an unwanted admirer. Carla's family lived there for five years. They moved to a much better house after I was able to feng shui the house, clear it and release the unwanted troublesome ghost.

Almost immediately, Carla was able to sleep without disruption. Her grades improved. She got a new job. Her mom and dad were able to move into a beautiful house. No more family arguments ensued and more business came in for both of them. They were able to take a vacation, which they had not done in years. Carla now has a job that she loves and, best of all, a new boyfriend came into her life. She is happily focused on entering college.

Letting the entity go was a very important step. I had gathered the important information that would help me determine what it would entail to release this wretched spirit from its lonely existence. Releasing it meant that the next family who moved in would be peaceful. Clearing out that spirit meant serenity and peace. We all deserve to have it. After all, our homes are our sanctuaries.

Chapter 21: Mamma

On October 23, 2006, my mother, Maria Luisina Cristofaro (ne Prezio), died. She had been living in Roggiano Gravina, Italy, the town where she was born. Two of my siblings and I wanted to see her. We learned of her sudden illness shortly before her passing. In haste, and hoping that we could be with her at her bedside, we rushed to get there. Knowing Mamma she did not want us to see her dying from a terminal illness. Instead, we saw her at Ospedale Lungro, the hospital chapel in Lungro, Italy, a remote area in Calabria, southern Italy.

It was a long journey. We were all exhausted travelers. When I first saw her from the doorway laid out in a casket, I could not get the courage to step over the chapel threshold. I froze. As I broke into tears and was not willing to go inside, I felt the presence of something pushing me to step in and so I did.

Yes, it was Mamma's physical body but her soul was absent in that place. That night we stayed at Mamma's house. It felt empty and solemn. I slept alone in the bedroom.

The experience I am about to tell you was the most profound of all. My mother appeared to me. She was beautiful, young, vibrant and happy. She was sitting on the small love seat across from my bed. She was not alone. Mamma was sitting next to her favorite brother, Amedeo. She was smiling, laughing at one point and telling my uncle that she was so happy that we came to see her. She looked very young with dark wavy hair and smooth alabaster skin. She was wearing a dress I had seen many times in old photos of her and my father.

My mother had a habit of slapping you when she got into a heavy laughter, and so her behavior was the same as she slapped my uncle's lap laughing, having fun and being happy. I knew that she was in a happy place and joyous. I was reminded of her infectious laughter and her love for her children and family. She was a great example of overcoming obstacles. I enjoyed seeing her beauty, grace and love. This image of her was a once in a lifetime gift that remains imbedded in my mind. I am so grateful to her for choosing me to see her.

The next morning I relayed the story to my brother, Franco, and sister, Clara. They listened intently and wanted to see her too. It was the morning of her funeral and we were getting ready for the church service.

In the kitchen next to the sink was a window. As I looked out there was a cat sitting on the grass staring at me. The cat was very still. It did not move at all for over an hour and sat in the same frozen position. Its coat was entirely pure white as Mamma's hair was and had prominent, very dark gray bushy eyebrows, as she had. I called my brother quietly to see this.

Was it my mother? I felt that it was. My mother was sending us the cat as a sign to let us know that she was present. As my brother looked out to see the cat, he also thought it was mamma saying

Mamma Cat (2006)

goodbye. My sister thought it was a comforting way for her to be among us, and so it was to be the beginning of her life-long presence in our lives.

It turns out to be true, because she continues to be around us. The cat lingered in stillness and sat there staring at us. We asked her friends and neighbors about it, and no one had ever seen a white cat, nor did my mother own a white cat. When we returned from the funeral the cat was not there and was never to be seen again.

EPILOGUE

Whether you have seen ghosts or entities or have felt them, there is a sense of wonder around it. We want to know and understand the world beyond ours. Some of us need to know what is going on with our close relatives and friends who have passed away. It's not a matter of religion or belief system that we hold. It's a matter of matter. Whether or not we believe in ghosts, our fascination remains, and will be a curiosity we want to quench.

We want to believe that with life there is an afterlife that exists. It gives us comfort to know that we can connect with our loved ones and also commune with them. Some of us have the ability to see them, and some of us have the ability to sense them and even feel their presence.

It's life. It's natural. It's not a weird idea.

Life goes on for us on earth and we want to believe that it also goes on in the afterlife as another way of doing and being whom we are and what we have accomplished. To take our essence with us gives us a hopeful belief in our existence. Even more, to actually make decisions based on the 'potential' of life after death or to judge the existence of entities is a subjective belief.

We can ignore the presence of ghosts and entities, but we cannot avoid the ever presence of their existence, because we are constantly reminded of them through our everyday encounters with the media. There are so many books on the subject of angels, spiritual guides, spirits, ghosts, entities and so many psychic and unexplained phenomena that no matter where we look, there they are in one form or another.

Denying their existence is not easy. Accepting their presence on earth is not a myth. Whether or not we want to believe or not believe in them is subjective.

Can we eradicate them, dismiss them, get rid of them altogether? After all, everything on this plane is a material manifestation. Can we erase life forms completely, totally? Can we manifest such apparitions if we really wanted to?

Life and death is a state of being. We could no more erase either one if we tried because we would be erasing our existence and our humanity. To believe or not to believe, that is the question. To some, the comfort of knowing that we can go to a place after we die and see our loved ones brings us closer to our higher power. If we choose to believe that there is such a being inside or outside of us, we can explain why it is that we existed in the first place. But either way, energy is matter and matter is energy. Vibration exists. It exists in everything and in all of us, great or small. Energy exists. All matter has vibration whether we see it or not. To some of us, that is all that is necessary to live our life and to have an open mind to all the possibilities that exist.

We cannot communicate, feel, know or commune with any matter or non-matter, if we do not open our minds at least to the possibility of its existence. We believe in the physical world, but do we believe in the metaphysical universe?

Appendices

Factors That Influence Our Success!

Change is inevitable but there are some things that we can change and some that we can't...Destiny, however, is fixed at birth and remains constant throughout our lives.

We can't change our destiny but we can change our attitudes, behaviors and our environment to make the most of our life.

FACTORS that *INFLUENCE* our *SUCCESS*:

1. DESTINY: your fate or destiny, your natal energy, your human potential

2. FENG SHUI: your energy, CHI flow in your environment

3. KARMA: your attitude, intentions, deeds, and beliefs

4. CULTIVATION: your efforts, education, self-improvement, and diligence

5. UNKNOWN: your life's luck whether it is auspicious or inauspicious.

Use them all to optimize your life!

10 Rules to a Serene & Ghost-Free Environment

1. **De-clutter is the number one rule for a productive, peaceful and serene environment.** Any type of clutter will invite spirits and promote ghost attraction. Keep all pathways clear, clean and spacious.
2. **Maintain your house(s), office(s) from the inside and outside.** Repair anything that is broken. Don't keep what you cannot use or need. Let it go. Be generous with your empty spaces.
3. **Do not live near or across from a funeral parlor, a cemetery, gravesite, dumpsite, or a hospital.** Even churches tend to attract spirits.
4. **Do not buy or live in a house built on sacred or consecrated ground.** Many houses that were built on ancient burial grounds have spirit energies.
5. **Use rock salt, preferably a coarse pure sea salt, in dark areas of your house, interior and exterior places, particularly from where you suspect noises are coming.** Place the salt in the Northeast and Southwest areas. Wind chimes should not be misplaced. Place them outside, especially in the

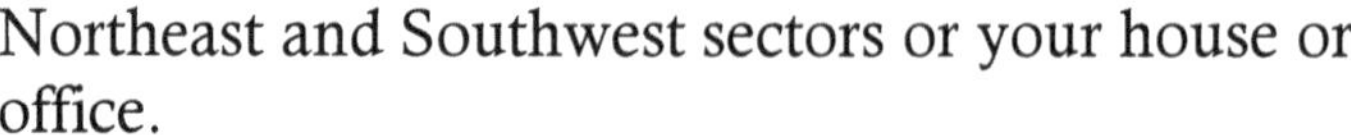

Northeast and Southwest sectors or your house or office.

6. **Keep your house and office well lit, airy and clean.** Dark, dingy, odorous, damp and unlit areas attract ghosts. Make sure your exteriors are well lit as well.

7. **Keep all dead things out of your house and office.** Ashes or remains of people, pets, and even dead plants, must be removed from your environment.

8. **Trees, shrubs, walls and fences too close to the house inhibit the flow of healthy chi energy.** Cut them back to allow sun to enter. Ghosts like to hide in weeping willow trees, so keep them far away from the house.

9. **A house that sits on an odd shaped lot is also not allowing energy to flow evenly.** Correct the lot by squaring it off with trees and shrubs.

10. **All houses built on steep slopes, stilts, hilltops and that drop away steeply on one side,** attract negative energy.

Make sure that if there is spirit or ghost activity in your environment that you contact a professional who can clear the negative energy from your home or office.

Glossary of Terms

BAGUA or PA KUA

The octagonal diagram of the 8 trigrams with one trigram on each side. These eight symbols are Chinese concepts c2100-1600 BC.

BRASCIERE

Made from brass or copper was filled with carbon for warmth and heat during winter cold months.

CALENDAR, SOLAR

Based on the earth's rotation around the Sun and the seasons.

CARDINAL POINTS

North, South, East and West directions.

CELEBRITIES

Today, feng shui is practiced by famous people like Donald Trump, Oprah Winfrey, Steven Spielberg, Richard Branson, Sting, and corporations like Coca-Cola, Sony, Shell, Procter & Gamble, Citibank and others. They actively embrace feng shui because it adds value to their service, increases their profitability, and creates harmonious relations among employees.

CENTO NERVI (piantagine maggiore)
Plantago major is a species of Plantago, family Plantaginaceae. The plant is native to most of Europe and Northern and Central Asia. Known as a common weed, it is known in English as Greater Plantain or Common Plantain.

The leaves are edible and used in herbal medicines, teas, to heal wounds, burns, snakebites and contains allantoin used as a replacement for hepatotoxic comfrey in preparations and as an antitoxin. Its also used in gardens and varieties come in purple and variegated leaves.

CHI, QI, CH'I
Life Force, energy flow, energy of the universe, sometimes referred to as cosmic breath or sky breath. Exists in every living thing. Chi also known as "qi" and "ch'i" is the universe life force. Chi is in all things, measurable and immeasurable, material and non-material and is everywhere. Chi is also referred to as the "dragon's breath." Feng shui translated is wind and water because when and where wind and water meet there is energy known as chi.

Sheng Chi is a positive harmonious flow. When used properly, feng shui allows for Sheng Chi to bring harmony to your environment and its affects are positive. Sha Chi is a negative, destructive force of energy flow that can result in illness, and negative outcomes.

There are many things that can reduce Sha Chi's effects. With simple solutions like opening a window to allow airflow, you can rid the stagnant chi, which will result in the reduction of Sha Chi.

Another way to open up flow of chi is to de-clutter your space. Clutter promotes offensive chi to reside in your home or office. Keep all your passageways clear and safe. Yang spaces improve chi flow. Good chi flow brings you abundance, good health and happy relationships and keeps out unwanted spirits.

CLEARING

Personal clearing is usually done by a dowser with a pendulum or a dowsing rod. Energy clearing is a type of kinesiology that frees up areas where stagnant energies are causing problems for the residents in the household.

COMPASS SCHOOL

Feng shui practice that uses the compass or lo pan to locate and diagnose the flow of chi energy.

DOWSING

A search for underground elements that affect a house and its occupants, sometimes by the use of a divining rod. Used to clear and renew energies in a structure or building.

EARTHLY BRANCHES

Rat, Dragon and Monkey (Water phase) to the North

Rabbit, Sheep and Boar (Wood phase) to the East

Horse, Dog and Tiger (Fire phase) to the South

Rooster, Ox and Snake (Metal phase) to the West

ELECTROMAGNETIC

Pertaining to or produced by magnetism which is developed by the passage of an electric current. An electric charge in motion producing electromagnetic energy.

ELEMENTS

The five elements used in feng shui are water, fire, earth, metal, and wood.

FACING DIRECTION

The front side of a building, often the side on which is the front door. Usually the side with a view.

FENG SHUI

The Art and Science of living your life in harmony with your environment. It is an ancient art related to the law and order of the universe and the power of nature. Feng shui is the metaphysical interpretation of your environment and the assessment of its predictable impact. It has been used for thousands of years as a way of balancing one's physical surroundings so that a person can absorb the maximum benefits of their home, while eliminating or reducing what would otherwise be the most threatening or negative features. Literally translated the words mean 'wind' and 'water'. These two natural forces influence QI or CH'I (both pronounced ch'i) the flow of energy around us. This ancient Chinese practice is a mathematical system that determines the most favorable direction for your living and working environment. Feng shui is not a religion, cult, superstition or magic.

FLYING STAR

A feng shui technique incorporating dimension of time. Measures flow of energy, quality and direction through calculation over time.

FORM SCHOOL

Feng shui practice that uses exterior land form structure to determine position of beneficial energies.

FOUR PILLARS

A person's personal Chinese astrological chart, using the eight Chinese characters and their association with elements. The chart is determined by the Stem and Branch of each of the year, month, day and hour of birth.

GEOMANCY

System of Divination. Interprets markings on the ground. Arabic system identifying markings in the sand. Often mistaken and mistranslated as feng shui.

GHOST

A disembodied spirit, soul of a dead person, wandering among the living and/or haunting living persons in a shadowy form. A demon, supernatural entity or a spirit appearing as a faint, displaced image. A ghost is the soul or spirit of a deceased person that appears or makes its presence known to the living. It is unearthly and a supernatural being, usually indicating good or bad intent toward a human being. It is also considered an apparition, phantom or poltergeist.

HSIA CALENDAR

Chinese traditional solar calendar also used for agriculture much like the almanac.

I CHING

The Chinese Book of Changes, based on 64 hexagrams, is a philosophical and divination method. Ancient in origin, describes all nature and human endeavor with regards to the interaction of yin and yang.

LO SHU

The magic square with 9 palaces, whose numbers add up to 15 in every direction. Basis for Flying Star Feng Shui.

LUCK

Comprised of three components; Heaven Luck or

fate, Earth Luck or feng shui and Man Luck or our own efforts.

METAPHYSICS

Branch of philosophy that examines the nature of reality including the relationship between mind and matter. Deals with the cause of matter and its opposite. Study of being and knowing.

PERIOD

A 20-year Period of time, nine of which make up a 180 year Great Cycle of time. Pertains to the Period of time the house or building was constructed. Each period has a certain fixed energy cycle.

SHA

Feng shui sha has three different meanings. One; killing, murder, slaughter, also called sha ch'i or killing ch'i. Two; sand, in geographical terms, small hill or hillside, site sha. Three; an evil sprit, as in three shas or fate stars. All distinguished by writing them in Chinese characters.

SHA CHI

Killing breath or killing Chi is a harmful energy directed at people and places. Negative surroundings and can be above ground or under ground. Saps energy and had detrimental effect. Pointed objects, noise, wires or overhead cables, proximity to a graveyard are just some of the negative affects called sha chi.

SHENG CHI AND SI CHI

Opposite sha chi. Most favorable energy generating success and prosperity location. Shen meaning spirit that enriches life and enlivens our physical body.

TAI SUI

Opposite Jupiter or Grand Duke Jupiter. In feng shui, the area of the house corresponding with the position of that year's tai sui is to be left undisturbed or misfortune will occur to the residents. Also called the Year Star.

THREE KILLINGS

Chinese san sha. Position is defined according to the four cardinal compass directions; North, South, East or West. Sits in the opposite direction spanning 90 degrees of the phase represented by the year's sign or earthly branch. Feng shui also advocates that you should never sit with your back to The Three Killings. Instead, you should sit facing it.

TRIGRAM

A sequence of three adjacent letters or symbols. The eight possible figures made of combinations of 3 broken and whole lines according to the *I CHING.*

WANG

Prosperous, empowering, vigorous.

WANG SHAN WANG SHUI

Flying Star configuration meaning prosperous mountain and prosperous water; this house chart is good for money and good for people. Considered the best feng shui house.

YANG

Male active principle. Opposite of yin, positive, bright, masculine.

YIN

Feminine passive energy, opposite of yang, with qualities of dark, damp, inside, negative, female.

Notes

www.ingramcontent.com/pod-product-compliance
Ingram Content Group UK Ltd.
Pitfield, Milton Keynes, MK11 3LW, UK
UKHW020125200726
13856UKWH00002B/740

9 781435 706408